THE
INTERWAR YEARS

The Spanish Civil War

Katie Griffiths

Cavendish
Square
New York

Published in 2018 by Cavendish Square Publishing, LLC
243 5th Avenue, Suite 136, New York, NY 10016

Library of Congress Cataloging-in-Publication Data

Names: Griffiths, Katie, author.
Title: The Spanish Civil War / Katie Griffiths.
Description: New York : Cavendish Square Publishing, [2018] |
Series: The interwar years | Includes bibliographical references and index.
Identifiers: LCCN 2016059804 (print) | LCCN 2017000070 (ebook) |
ISBN 9781502627193 (library bound) | ISBN 9781502627162 (E-book)
Subjects: LCSH: Spain--History--Civil War, 1936-1939--Juvenile literature.
Classification: LCC DP269 .G69 2018 (print) | LCC DP269 (ebook) | DDC 946.08/1--dc23
LC record available at https://lccn.loc.gov/2016059804

Editorial Director: David McNamara
Editor: Kristen Susienka
Copy Editor: Alex Tessman
Associate Art Director: Amy Greenan
Designer: Alan Sliwinski
Production Coordinator: Karol Szymczuk
Photo Research: J8 Media

Printed in the United States of America

Contents

Setting the Stage for Spain

F ought in Spain from 1936 to 1939, the Spanish Civil War was one of the bloodiest and most destabilizing internal conflicts of the twentieth century. For four years, the country ripped itself apart, and the effects of this struggle would later influence an even more severe global crisis: World War II. In many ways, the Spanish Civil War was shaped and set in motion by its predecessor, World War I. However, the conflict was fundamentally a battle of deep-seated internal issues, namely surrounding Spain's political factions and economic hardships.

Background to War

During the 1930s, Spain's political landscape was deeply divided between right-wing Nationalists and left-wing

Opposite: *The Spanish Civil War turned ordinary citizens into soldiers and guerrilla fighters.*

Republicans. The Nationalist Party was composed of monarchists, landowners, employers, members of the Roman Catholic Church, and soldiers in the army. In contrast, the Republicans were workers, trade unions, socialists, and peasants. Spain was suffering the widespread effects of the United States' Great Depression, which began after the Wall Street crash in October 1929. That same year, partly as a result of this turmoil, the military dictatorship that had ruled Spain since 1923 collapsed. Two years later, the king of Spain left the country, thinking this would prevent full-out civil war, and the Republican Party took power.

Over the next five years, the Republican and Nationalist Parties continually jostled each other for greater political control of the country, and both had periods as Spain's elected government. The nation became increasingly unstable and chaotic. Then, in 1936, the army rebelled and forcibly removed the then-Republican government from power. Civil war had arrived.

Despite the internal nature of the war, Spain was closely watched by the rest of Europe. Within its borders, the fate of Fascism was being played out, and other nations were fully aware that the war's outcome would affect the next major conflict within the continent. If Spain were to fall under the Fascist flag, then France would be surrounded by Fascist neighbors; it was already flanked by Fascist Italy, led by Benito Mussolini, and Germany, led by Adolf Hitler. Should France be invaded by one of these neighbors, then the alliances of other anti-Fascist nations would be severely weakened, and there would be one less ally to fight against Hitler and Mussolini's plans to expand their own borders.

Spain also controlled important military resources—in particular, a strategic naval base on the Mediterranean Sea and the Atlantic Ocean. If the base came under Fascist control it would allow the regimes to control shipping and act as a launching pad for Fascist submarines, both severe blows that would put military and economic pressure on other European countries.

Religion lay at the heart of Spanish society and public life.

Influential Factors

Though politics were a crucial aspect of the eventual Spanish Civil War, there were many other elements that contributed to the state of instability and public aggression responsible for moving Spain into violent chaos and military action.

Agriculture

In the first half of the twentieth century, Spanish industry was dominated by agriculture. It was the country's primary industry and main avenue of export, and Spain was highly dependent on its revenues. However, the system of land and landowning was still rather feudal. Wealthy families, based mainly in the south of Spain, owned large private estates known as *latifundias*. These areas were in turn farmed by landless laborers. Wages were extremely low. Roughly only seven thousand owners controlled more than 15 million acres (6 million hectares) of land. In the north, farms were often much smaller and less economically viable. It is believed that half of the laborers used on Spain's farms lived on the edge of starvation. Once the granary of the Roman Empire, Spain now had the lowest agricultural productivity of any nation in Europe.

The Military

The political clout of the army had grown dramatically in the last century, and so had its ranks. However, instead of a well-resourced and well-disciplined unit, it had become a

By the war's outbreak, the military was overfunded and underregulated. Here, Nationalists kiss the Spanish flag, showing their loyalty.

grossly over-staffed officer corps, with roughly one general to every hundred poorly equipped soldiers. The majority of the military's budget went to the officers' comfort and salaries rather than outfitting ground-level troops. This also led the organization to become more conservative, and its increased sense of confidence made it prone to interfering in national politics.

Religion

For many centuries, the Catholic Church was a fundamental staple of Spanish life. Over time it accumulated huge levels of wealth and power, which many greatly resented. The authority of the Church was closely identified with the wealthy classes and intensely conservative in its outlook.

As a result, it became seen as an obstacle to concrete social change. Despite the fact the majority of Spaniards did not attend Catholic services, called masses, there was a strong religious following in the south.

The Church permeated all aspects of life and held a particularly firm monopoly on education. This meant the Church also had a huge influence on the values and knowledge passed on to Spain's next generation, allowing them to continually cement their own position. Amongst several factions of society, it was believed that restricting the power of the Church was crucial to creating a fairer Spain.

Internal Borders

The geography of Spain shows a land divided by rivers and mountain ranges. In between these areas there were distinct groups that developed their own dialects—some even their own languages—and own cultures. Areas such as the Basque country and Catalonia wanted independence and control of their own affairs. Generally, Republicans were far more sympathetic to the demands of such groups, especially the Catalans; however, Nationalists were fervently opposed on the grounds that allowing the territories their own autonomy would weaken Spain.

Key Players

Many people were involved both in the creation of the conflict and its continuance. However, two men in particular held great influence over the civil war's outcome: Miguel Primo de Rivera and Francisco Franco. Both military dictators, their actions changed the face of twentieth-century Spain and continue to echo beyond.

Primo de Rivera

Shortly after World War I, economic depression had led to strikes and unrest throughout Spain. Coupled with military defeats in Morocco, this tension led in 1923 to the emergence of a right-wing military dictatorship under the command of Miguel Primo de Rivera. His rule was initially reform-oriented; however, later on, his regime's popularity fell away. Primo de Rivera was forced to resign in 1930 after losing the support of the army. The following year municipal elections were held with the vast majority of voters calling for the establishment of a republic. They also demanded the king, Alfonso XIII, abdicate, but he refused. Overwhelmed, however, the king eventually left Spain on April 14, 1931. A republic was declared with Niceto Alcalá-Zamora as provisional prime minister.

General Franco

Francisco Franco was born in 1892 in the northwest Spanish naval town of Ferrol. In 1907 he entered the military academy in Toledo. His first posting came in 1912, where he was sent to join a **colonial** war in Morocco. He quickly gained a reputation for bravery and competence, winning rapid promotions, and by 1920 he had reached the position of second in command

General Francisco Franco would become the face of the Spanish Civil War.

of the Foreign Legion. Just six years later he was promoted to brigadier general, becoming the youngest in Europe to hold such a post. His military exploits made him a national hero and a favorite of King Alfonso XIII.

Franco was vehemently opposed to the forced exit of the monarchy in 1931. As a Nationalist, he firmly believed in the sanctity of the crown. Despite his opposition to the republic, he was posted to the Balearic Islands, a position that was above his rank. Yet Franco was still angry. It seemed clear to him that he was purposely being given posts he did not want. Though his position was higher than ever, the government was maneuvering him to places where they believed he could not cause them trouble. In 1934, he was promoted to major general and later he viciously crushed a miner's revolt in Asturias. His actions included mass executions of strikers, including women and children. By 1935, Franco was made commander in chief of the Spanish armed forces in Morocco and chief of staff for the entire Spanish army.

In the war years, he would become notorious and would eventually rise to power, having a significant impact on Spanish life, livelihood, and history.

Countdown to Conflict

Between 1931 and 1933, the Republican government, attempting to reform the country, brought in measures aimed at limiting the power of the Church. The Jesuits were disbanded and church and state became officially separated. The government also instituted civil marriage and allowed divorce. It also sought to address regional issues by granting Catalonia autonomy. However, it failed to bring forth any serious land reforms. This led to a weakening of support in rural areas. Finally, it gutted the officer corps of the military, and thousands of officers were forced to retire on half pay. This caused major resentment amongst the army.

In 1932, General José Sanjurjo of the Spanish army attempted to lead a military revolt and was crushed by government forces. He would later become a chief conspirator in the Nationalist rising that led to the civil war. However, this incident revealed to the country the depth of anger within the military toward the new republic. This resentment was echoed by right-wing elements in Spanish society. The Republican government's measures against the Church offended those who believed Catholicism to be at the heart of Spanish civilization. The politician Alcalá-Zamora resigned in protest. He was replaced as prime minister by the **anticlerical** liberal Manuel Azaña Díaz. As a result of the government's actions, two things happened. First, the right-wing Catholic Confederación Española de Derecha Autónomas (CEDA) Party was formed, led by Catholic José María Gil Robles.

Second, a Fascist Party under the leadership of Primo de Rivera's son, José Antonio, was established. They called themselves the Falange Party.

Toward the end of 1933, support for the Republican Party had waned dramatically and in November a new right-wing government was elected. This fresh power immediately set to work reversing the reforms of the previous administration and canceling measures placed against the Church. The period between 1933 and 1935 became known by those on the left as the "Two Black Years" as reform after reform was pushed back. In 1934, a general strike was called against the government. As a result, mass arrests followed and left-wing newspapers were closed. The statute granting Catalonia autonomy was suspended and Spanish politics became fiercely polarized.

In 1936, an election was called and a Popular Front of Communists, socialists, Republicans, and separatists formed in opposition to the right-wing government. Right-wing parties garnered a National Front in response. The Popular Front was convinced a right-wing victory would lead directly to Fascism, and the National Front believed equally strongly that a Popular Front victory would lead to a **Bolshevik** revolution in Spain. In the end, the Popular Front narrowly won the election and Manuel Azaña Díaz was appointed president with Santiago Casares Quiroga as prime minister.

The new administration attempted to reintroduce the reforms undone by the previous government, and disorder and political violence quickly spread through Spain. Rural workers and peasants seized land by force. There were numerous strikes. The ranks of the Falange grew dramatically as disillusioned supporters of the more moderate CEDA flocked to their banner. With increased confidence, the Falange used greater and greater political violence, and attacks and counterattacks between right-wing and left-wing supporters became more frequent.

As the political storm raged throughout Spain, the army began plotting to finally overthrow the government once and for all. The generals firmly believed in monarchy and were increasingly alarmed by the growing influence of socialists and **anarchists** in Spanish politics. The plot was led by General Emilio Mola.

On July 13, Republican police assassinated the monarchist politician José Calvo Sotelo in revenge for the murder of a colleague by Falangists. Sotelo had been an outspoken critic of the second republic and a leading member of the anti-Republican radical right. The Republican government began an investigation into the murder, but no conclusion was ever reached. Mola and his comrades had been planning their uprising for February; however, the government's lack of concern or initiative gave them a useful opportunity.

Using this incident as a pretext, the generals quickly mobilized their forces. The revolt began on July 17 in Spanish Morocco under the joint command of Mola, Francisco Franco, José Sanjurjo, and Gonzalo Queipo de Llano. This uprising marked the beginning of civil war.

Conflict in Context

I n the years preceding the Spanish Civil War, Spain was a country torn between the opposing forces of tradition and progress. Fragmented by numerous voices, it was a society unable to come together to find common ground and a single solution to its many issues and insecurities. This anxiety affected every section of life: the monarchy, the government, the military, and the economy. All of these aspects were unstable, divided, outspoken, rebellious, or depressed, providing unease and tension. Added to this mixture was a conservative upper class, an angry and starving working class, and a progressive middle class.

As Spain met each new challenge, such as the loss of its colonial empire or the entrance of World War I, different issues and groups were ignited and forced the country toward an increasingly split society. The conflict itself was

Opposite: *Before the war, Spanish society had become severely divided both politically and economically.*

not inevitable—very few things in history truly are—however, the events leading to 1936 would eventually set Spain on a collision course with itself.

Background and Context: The Nineteenth Century

In times of political and economic uncertainty, societies often begin to question their own way of life and look for radical change. Spain was no different. Throughout the nineteenth century, the country had veered between a constitutional monarchy and an absolute monarchy. A constitutional monarchy is a form of rule where the king or queen exercises their power in accordance with a written or unwritten constitution. Their authority is not boundless and they must act within the limits set by an established legal framework. An absolute monarchy, on the other hand, as its name suggests, is not restricted in the same way. The monarch or sovereign is free to exercise their authority over both people and government in whatever way they see fit. The shifting between two radically different forms of rule left both Spain's government and its people unsettled and insecure. This not only weakened the country's political and economic stability but also left space for the possibility of a different form of governance.

The nineteenth century saw one of the biggest struggles for control of Spain's political future. The insecure nature of the country's highest authority, its monarch, was reflected down the political chain. In its simplest form, the key struggle was between conservatives and liberals, as each party attempted revolution and **counterrevolution** to further their own ideals. Liberals primarily wanted to reform Spain's government, its

King Amadeo I was intended to return stability to Spain.

parliament called the **Cortes**, and limit the power of the monarchy in order to establish a liberal state.

This was not an entirely new or radical idea. The goal of a liberal state was first begun in 1812 with Spain's first constitution. This guaranteed universal male suffrage, a constitutional monarchy, and freedom of the press, among other ideals. Conservatives, conversely, were concerned with preserving tradition, and upholding the power and position of the monarchy and the Catholic Church. They struggled with liberals in the government throughout the century to prevent the passage of radical or progressive legislation.

Turmoil and Uprisings

The initial progressive streak of the nineteenth century— with the passing of the 1812 constitution and the reforms brought in by the liberal government of 1820–1823—lost momentum when, in 1823, King Ferdinand VII dissolved the constitution and ended the radical liberal government. This was only the first in a series of major power shifts within the country.

Between 1814 and 1874 there were twelve successful coups. One of the most notable occurred in 1868, when an uprising unseated the new sovereign, Queen Isabella II, daughter of Ferdinand VII. Prior to this, the country had been racked with urban riots. A growing liberal movement amongst the middle classes and the military was becoming increasingly concerned with the monarchy's **ultra-conservatism**, so they decided to take action. The Spanish Revolution of 1868 was primarily led by General Juan Prim. Also known as the Glorious Revolution, the uprising began with a naval mutiny at Cádiz. Forces under the command of admiral Juan Bautista Topete rebelled against the monarchy and government. This was quickly followed by General Prim and Francisco Serrano denouncing the government publicly. This led much of the army to defect to the rebel generals.

Isabella attempted to stand her ground with a quick, decisive naval victory. However, her loyal forces were soundly defeated at the Battle of Alcolea, and the queen herself fled to France. Thus, Spain moved again into radical liberal hands; however, the revolutionary elements behind the coup lacked direction and once more the country plunged into confusion. Finally, General Francisco Serrano was installed as regent until a suitable replacement for Isabella could be found. In 1869, the Cortes drew up their first truly liberal constitution since 1812, marking a new era in Spanish governance.

By 1870, the government had selected Italian prince Amadeo to take over Spain's monarchy. Amadeo was duke of Aosta and had support from Prim and Serrano; however, despite his royal background and strong credentials, he had almost no experience as a ruler.

Difficulties began almost immediately, among which included the assassination of Amadeo's main supporter, General Prim, on the day of the king's election. Thus during his reign, Amadeo was only able to count on the support of progressive members of the Cortes, and even these members were divided in their opinions over the extent of monarchical power. In addition, there were a number of **Carlist** and Republican uprisings in the few years following Amadeo's ascension. Crucially, he failed to gain popular support among the Spanish people. Faced with such difficulties, Amadeo abdicated after reigning only three years, claiming that the Spanish people were "ungovernable."

In choosing to vacate the monarchy, Amadeo offered the Spanish people a unique opportunity. He effectively paved the way for the first Spanish republic. This, however, did not increase stability, and the new republic was soon under siege from numerous quarters. Carlists launched a violent insurrection in response to a poor outcome in the 1872 elections; the International Workingmen's Association began calling for a socialist revolution; the regions of Navarre and Catalonia witnessed revolts and escalating violence; and the Catholic Church used its influence to place further pressure on the government. This perfect storm led to the swift dissolution of the republic after less than a year. The House of Bourbon was once again established as Spain's monarchy, and political power swung back toward conservatives and traditional values.

Yet this did not please many of the republic's critics either. Both Carlist and anarchist groups emerged in opposition of the monarchy. Carlists, while pro-monarchy, favored the establishment of Don Carlos Maria Alfonso Marcelo de Borbón-Dos Sicilias y de Borbón-Parma, Infante of Spain and the Duke of Calabria, and his descendants as sovereign, and fought to promote traditional Spanish and Catholic values. Supporters of anarchism were primarily found among the working class, and the movement was stronger in Spain than in any other European country at the time. Yet despite national anger toward the upper classes and the popularity of the movement, anarchists were often easily defeated in clashes with government forces.

The Issue of Monarchy

The monarchy was one of Spain's biggest issues in the lead up to the Spanish Civil War. By the end of the nineteenth century, the monarchy was perceived to be a major source of Spain's ineffectuality. Power struggles between conservatives and liberals in the Cortes often centered around the desire or refusal to place limits on sovereign power. Many liberals did not trust the monarchy, believing that the king or queen would serve only his or her own interests and not the people's. The Bourbon dynasty, to which Queen Isabella II belonged, operated as part of a two-party monarchial system known as turnismo. This organization placed the monarch at the top, as head of state, and also required a constant rotation of liberal and conservative governments. First, the liberal government would be in power, then the conservative, and so on. While its supporters believed this was a fair system that allowed both sides of Spain's political field to represent the people, there were equal numbers that wished to reform the system or destroy it entirely.

Adding to this instability was the personal actions of individual monarchs. Depending on where their own political leanings fell, they were capable of bolstering an unpopular regime or weakening a ruling party. Queen Isabella II continually switched her support between liberal and conservative factions, causing mistrust, suspicion, and even outrage between moderates and progressives. Her grandson, King Alfonso XIII, supported Primo de Rivera, essentially tying the monarchy's survival to the popularity of a dictator, and when Primo de Rivera eventually fell from grace, Alfonso was left without popular support or political allies.

The monarchy's failure to connect with an increasingly impoverished and frustrated population also affected the country's interaction with and perception of World War I. While Alfonso was praised internationally for his humanitarian efforts during this period, the country's neutrality angered many of its citizens, who firmly believed that Spain should take a more active role in the conflict.

Money and Power

Another key issue of nineteenth-century Spain was the economy. Some historians have argued that the roots of the Spanish Civil War lie in the century's traditional distribution of economic wealth and power. During this period, land and wealth was concentrated among the *latifundia*. These were owners of large estates who possessed the majority of Spain's resources and industry.

As the gap between the Spanish aristocracy and the rest of the country widened, ordinary Spaniards became more discontented.

It was this century where Spain saw the loss of its colonial empire as territories gained freedom or turned against their imperial oppressors. The loss of this previous wealth soon reduced the country to one of Europe's poorest and least-developed nations. By 1850, over three-quarters of the population were illiterate, and there was very little industry except for the production of textiles in Castille. Spain possessed a healthy supply of the iron and coal necessary for industrial development, but this was located in the north and northeast of the country and was difficult to transport across the vast plain of the central Iberian Peninsula.

In addition to a severe lack of rivers viable for transportation, the country had only a rudimentary road system. British industrialists were brought over to teach Spanish laborers how to extract iron ore and to investigate the possibility of building a national railway network. However, when construction of the network was at last completed, it simply ran outward from Madrid and bypassed major centers of natural resources.

Economic limitations also hampered Spain's growth. High tariffs were placed on basic goods such as grain, while simultaneously cheap foreign imports were almost entirely banned. The eastern provinces were forced to pay high prices for domestic cereals transported with great difficulty over the peninsula, while cheap Italian grain could have been far more easily imported by ship. In previous decades, Spain had been a major exporter. However, due to the rise of British industry, the country could now no longer keep up. By the end of the nineteenth century, the country's few exports were mainly agricultural products. Catalonia continued to be Spain's one center of industry, but Castille remained its political and cultural center, preventing any major political change in favor of the working classes.

The First World War

In July 1914, Europe was plunged into World War I. A global conflict spanning multiple continents, this war was fought between the Allied Powers of France, Britain, Russia, Serbia,

Montenegro, Belgium, Japan, Italy, Portugal, Romania, Hejaz, the United States, Greece, and Siam, against the Central Powers of Germany, Austria-Hungary, the Ottoman Empire, and Bulgaria. Other smaller parties would also join both sides for shorter periods of time. The fighting lasted just over four years, lasting from July 28, 1914, to November 11, 1918. It began with the assassination of Archduke Franz Ferdinand of Austria and ended with an Allied victory and the downfall of the German, Russian, Ottoman, and Austro-Hungarian empires. In just four years, the power balance of Europe was drastically altered, as were the fates of many countries around the world.

Spain's Position

Throughout World War I, Spain remained neutral and refused to become embroiled in the conflict. It had enjoyed neutrality during the tensions of Europe's prewar period and was determined to continue this. It quickly became one of the most important neutral countries on the continent, being a significant source of goods for France, the other Allies, and South America, where it still held colonies. Spain would have no direct military involvement during the war; however, German forces were **interned** in the Spanish-held territory of Guinea in late 1915.

On the day that war broke across Europe, Spain's conservative prime minister, Eduardo Dato, stood in the Cortes to officially declare Spain's neutrality and was applauded by his colleagues. Yet public opinion was divided, and despite the official stance, the Spanish people were less convinced. The upper classes, the Catholic Church and the Spanish Army publicly favored the Central Powers with a particular favoritism shown toward Germany. This **Germanophile** tendency was also seen in political circles, represented by the reactionary Carlists and revolutionary Mauristas. Mauristas were followers of the former prime minister Antonio Maura, who ironically favored closer tries with the Allies. Pro-Allied sentiment was found mainly amongst the middle and professional classes and intellectuals, as well as Catalan Nationalists, Republicans, and socialists. A number of liberals, including leader of the opposition Álvaro de Figueroa, were also Pro-Allied. The vast majority of Pro-Allied supporters favored France of all the Allied forces.

Spanish Economy and Military

To a certain extent, the war reaped a number of benefits for Spain. Demand for Spanish goods grew and its gold reserves more than tripled as violence raged through Europe. Industry in the north and east of the country expanded with demand, and the government was able to use this financial boost to pay back a significant amount of its national debt.

Yet the country quickly found that these small gains were offset by major losses. The inflow of capital into Spain led to widespread **inflation** and imports dropped significantly. The loss of cheap basic commodities from abroad exacerbated poverty levels in rural areas and the south. This shortage

The military attempted to block any attempts to curtail its freedoms or finances.

eventually became known as the *crisis de subsistencias*. This growth in poverty intensified the migration of rural workers to industrial areas and the substandard railway network was unable to bear the increased demand. By 1915 food riots had broken out in several cities, and in December of that year, the government was forced to resign. They were replaced by a more liberal government under the leadership of Álvaro de Figueroa.

July 1916 saw the joining of two major socio-political forces: the Unión General de Trabajadores and the Confederación Nacional del Trabajo. The organizations were Spain's two main trade unions, though they each operated under different political ideologies. The Unión operated under socialist principles, while the Confederación perused an anarcho-syndicalist agenda. The union of the two was designed to place pressure on the government and its employment policies. They even threatened a widespread general strike in March 1917.

Spain saw further damage to its industry through the war maneuvers of its neighbors. Despite King Alfonso XIII's protesting of Germany's use of submarines, by the end of the war Spain had lost 140,000 tons (127,000 metric tons) of shipping to the U-boat activity.

The example of the trade unions inspired not only ordinary workers but also Spain's military. The officers formed their own union, the Junta de Defensa Nacional. The aim of this organization was to block the passage of a piece of legislation known as the bill of military reform. This bill was designed to professionalize the military using measures such as intellectual and physical tests as determiners for promotions. The government had intended to use the legislation to heavily downscale the ranks of the officers' corps. Angered by the government's actions, the Junta protested and demanded the traditional promotion and pay system based strictly on seniority.

The Path to Civil War

The frequent oscillation of government and the growing anger of an impoverished nation finally led to a military coup in 1923, which saw the rise of Miguel Primo de Rivera. With this action the country transitioned to a military dictatorship. He firmly believed that it was politicians who were responsible for the ruination of Spain. However,

MIGUEL PRIMO DE RIVERA

Miguel Primo de Rivera was an aristocrat and military officer who became dictator of Spain. He was born on January 8, 1870, and served in office from September 15, 1923, to January 28, 1930. He was extremely critical of Spain's politicians and believed that he alone could restore the nation.

He came to power in 1923 after a coup where he was supported by both King Alfonso XIII and the army. He was quickly appointed to the position of prime minister by the king and promised to eliminate corruption within Spanish politics, as well as regenerate Spain's stagnant industry. During his first few months in office, he suspended the constitution, established martial law, imposed strict censorship laws, and outlawed alternative political parties.

Very little social reform took place under Primo de Rivera; however, he did attempt to reduce unemployment through the building of public works. To raise the necessary funds, he imposed high taxes on the rich, but after they protested he quickly changed tact and used public loans. This caused immediate and rapid inflation. He lost the support of the army and was forced to resign in January 1930.

Three years later, Primo de Rivera's eldest son, José Antonio, founded the extreme right-wing Falange Party, a Fascist organization that would play a major role in the Spanish Civil War. José and his brother were arrested by government forces in 1936 and later executed by Republican soldiers after the war's outbreak.

Following the establishment of Franco's brutal and authoritarian regime in 1939, many Spaniards reconsidered their perspectives on Primo de Rivera, and he became regarded more fondly in comparison.

history has often seen him as an inept leader who lacked the political skill to rebuild the country. During his reign, he alienated his major supporters, such as the army, and failed to build popular support among general voters, relying instead on the upper classes. His failures discredited Spain's monarchy and increased social tensions within the country. He finally resigned in January 1930 as the last of his support faded.

Primo de Rivera was later replaced by General Dámaso Berenguer, who was in turn succeeded by Admiral Juan Bautista Aznar-Cabañas. Both of Primo de Rivera's successors would continue his example of rule by decree.

During this time, public support for the monarchy declined rapidly. The populace called for the reestablishment of a republic and demanded municipal elections to be held that April. The provincial capitals were won almost exclusively by socialist and liberal Republicans. After Primo de Rivera's government resigned, the king fled Spain and the second Spanish republic was officially established.

The Second Republic

The revolutionary force that swept into power with the arrival of the second republic was headed by Niceto Alcalá-Zamora. It quickly established a provisional government with Alcalá-Zamora as president and head of state. The venture started with moderate success and the republic had broad support from all sections of society, but it wasn't long before problems arose.

President Niceto Alcalá-Zamora was swept into power with the rise of the second republic.

The first crack in the glass occurred in May 1931 after a violent attack outside a pro-monarchy club. The result was a rash of anticlerical violence that swept throughout Madrid and southwest Spain. The right demanded justice and security from the Republican government, but the administration was slow to react. Their lack of action angered right-wing supporters and seemed to be further proof that the republic not only sanctioned violence against the Church but would persecute its followers in the future.

As the country moved into June and July, the conflict mutated, with the Confederación Nacional del Trabajo (CNT) calling for several strikes. This led to bloody confrontations between CNT members and the civil guard and resulted in a harsh crackdown by civil guard and army forces against the CNT in Seville. The brutality of the reaction convinced many of the working classes that the Republican administration was as dictatorial as the monarchy itself. In response, the CNT union announced their intention to overthrow its power through revolution. However, the following year's elections saw the return of many Republicans and socialists to the Cortes. In an attempt to pull back popular support and deal with the acute poverty of rural Spain, the government instituted an eight-hour working day and gave land tenure to farm workers.

The Threat of Fascism

Despite the reforms pushed through by the second republic government, Fascism remained a lurking threat. Its appeal grew primarily on the back of controversial reforms, such as the limiting of the military's resources and autonomy. In December 1931, the Cortes declared a new reformist, liberal, and democratic constitution. Building on previous work, the document promised strong provisions for the enforcement of secularization among other items.

During this period, Spain was still a deeply religious country and this move alienated many moderates who were committed Catholics. The Republican government's influence sank further at the 1931 elections when Manuel Azaña became prime minister of a minority government, leaving the liberal government with less power to push through legislation. Within two years, the right had gained the popular support the left had lost.

In the 1933 elections, right-wing parties swept to victory due to a number of issues. First and foremost was the fact that anarchist supporters had been absent from voting. Likewise, there was increased right-wing resentment of the incumbent government due to controversial land reform decrees. In addition to this, several right-wing groups had formed an alliance under the name CEDA. This cooperation helped to collect right-wing votes and push for Nationalist candidates. Another significant aspect was the introduction of female voters, who largely endorsed center-right parties.

Two Black Years

The final period that led directly to the outbreak of civil war became known as the "Two Black Years." This was a time that changed Spain forever and made civil war inevitable.

As a result of the 1933 elections, a new government had been formed under Alejandro Lerroux of the Radical Republican Party (RRP). He reversed many of the reforms brought in under the previous administration, in deals that largely benefited the landowning classes. In addition, Lerroux pardoned all agitators involved in an unsuccessful uprising led by General José Sanjurjo in August 1932, as well as removing price controls that contributed to widespread malnutrition among Spain's populace.

The political divide within Spain deepened and a number of pro-monarchy supporters arose. Among them was the Fascist-Nationalist Falange Party, or Falange Española y de las JONS. The party was founded in October 1933 by José Antonio, the son of Miguel Primo de Rivera. The organization's mission was to stand against socialism, Marxism, capitalism, and republicanism. In particular, it supported the establishment of a Fascist state in Spain, similar to the contemporary regime in Italy led by Benito Mussolini.

By the end of 1934, there was open violence on Spain's streets and militancy increased tenfold. It is believed that over three hundred people were assassinated following the 1933 elections, and more than fifteen hundred were wounded in political violence. The unstable liberal government faced opposition from both the left and the right as both sides became more extreme and outspoken. Public opinion increasingly favored radical revolution over peaceful democratic negotiation, and the number of political riots and acts of vandalism rose dramatically. The final months of that year saw two government collapses bringing more and more members of the Fascist CEDA Party into the government.

Meanwhile, representatives in Catalonia, angered by the region's poverty and the government's abuse, attempted to declare the region an independent state operating within Spanish borders. The territory remained autonomous and highly unstable politically throughout the war. After the Nationalists had taken power in Spain, Catalonia would be stripped of its autonomy and its culture harshly repressed.

In Asturias, miners and other workers staged an armed uprising against the right-wing CEDA Party. A then-unknown general named Francisco Franco was sent to suppress the workers, and his troops killed men, women, and children before carrying out summary executions of the region's populace. Roughly one thousand people died in the conflict, with less than 250 deaths of government troops. Franco and his comrade, General Manuel Goded Llopis, were lauded as heroes.

The cabinet went through another collapse with more positions passed on to CEDA members. Farmers' wages were again reduced and the military purged of Republican supporters. Franco was made chief of staff.

In 1935, Azaña and Indalecio Prieto worked to reunify the left in the run up to the 1936 election. They held rallies in a movement that would eventually become known as the Popular Front.

The right-wing government collapsed after two internal scandals and the Popular Front won the 1936 election, despite having vastly smaller resources. In the wake of its crushing defeat, the political right moved from making plans to take control of the republic to overthrowing it entirely.

MANUEL AZAÑA DÍAZ

Manuel Azaña Díaz was the second prime minister of the second Spanish republic. He served from 1931 to 1933, and then later in 1936. He also served as president during the Spanish Civil War.

Heavily critical of the conservative Nationalists, Azaña was outspoken against the state from early on in his political career. In 1924 he published a manifesto against both King Alfonso and Primo de Rivera's dictatorship, and in 1930 he signed the Pact of San Sebastián, which unified all Spanish republican and regionalist parties against both Primo de Rivera and the king. When Alcalá-Zamora was elected prime minister of the provisional government of the republic in April 1931, he initially named Azaña as minister of war. However, by October, Alcalá-Zamora had officially resigned his position to become president of the republic, and Azaña took his place, leading a coalition of left-wing parties and socialists.

Azaña was instrumental in bringing through key Republican reforms. He introduced work accident insurance, reduced the size of the Spanish army, and worked to reduce the power and influence of the Roman Catholic Church in Spain. This included abolishing Church-operated schools and charities in favor of state-run secular schools. Under his leadership, the Cortes enacted an **agrarian** reform program, which ensured that large private landholdings were confiscated and redistributed among the rural poor.

However, Azaña's reforms only went so far. He was not a socialist and the agrarian reform program was not only badly written, but very little effort was made to actually carry it out. He did little to reform Spain's taxation system to shift the burden onto the wealthy. Instead, the government continued to support the owners of industry against workers' strikes. Lastly, his extreme anti-clericalism alienated many of his supporters. Spain was still deeply Catholic, and Azaña's reforms alarmed moderates within his party.

After the conclusion of the war and the defeat of the republic, he fled to France, resigned his office, and died in exile in 1940.

Despite the increase in popular support, Azaña's government was weak and internal conflicts led to a lack of clear political direction and an inability to either push through much-needed legislation or create greater political harmony. Azaña became increasingly isolated and was eventually voted out by right-wing elements within the government. His removal has often been cited by historians as one of the major steps toward revolution and civil war.

In the final months before the conflict, the Falange Party worked to create increased militancy on Spain's streets. Despite Prieto's efforts to promote a series of public works and civil order reforms, the mood of the country had moved beyond such actions. The political divides within the Popular Front weakened the government in acting against right-wing militancy, and both sides of the government were under public attack from Falange and socialist pressure groups.

Prieto attempted to warn the government and military against rumors of a conspiracy involving several Spanish generals but was ignored or discounted. That was until the fateful day of July 17, 1936.

The Path
of Civil War

2

ollowing a period of instability and political crisis
in the second Spanish republic, a group of military
officers organized a military coup against the Popular
Front government elected in February 1936. Planning
began early that year and the coup was launched first in the
Spanish colony of Morocco and then in Spain proper over
July 17 and 18. However, what was intended to be a swift and
decisive takeover failed, leaving the country divided between
government-controlled and rebel-controlled areas, and civil
war ensued.

The Coup

Collaborating with officers both in the colonies and within
Spain, the rebels planned the uprising to begin at 5 a.m. in

Opposite: *Clashes between Republicans and General Franco's
forces began in 1936. Here, Republicans fight using trench warfare,
circa 1936.*

Spanish Morocco with factions in Spain proper to revolt exactly one day later. Staggering these events would allow troops to head back to Spain to assist with the risings there.

Rebel control of Morocco was almost certain. Its thirty-thousand-strong Army of Africa was Spain's most elite and professional military force. Many of its soldiers were mercenaries and its officers loyal to the military rather than the government. In addition to this, a large number of its forces had been recruited from the local Muslim population, who were angry with the rumor that the Spanish government wished to abolish Islam.

As the uprisings spread to Spain, the coup's swift progress began to unravel. Rebels seized Cádiz and Seville, but the government retained control of most of the country, including major centers such as Málaga, Jaén, and Almería. In Madrid, Nationalist forces were hemmed into the Montaña barracks, which fell to much bloodshed. On July 19, the newly appointed prime minister, José Giral, ordered weapons to be distributed to the unions in defense against the rebels in Madrid, Barcelona, and Valencia. Anarchists used these weapons to occupy large parts of Aragon and Catalonia. One rebel leader, General Goded, was captured in Barcelona and condemned to death.

As the smoke cleared, the pieces were laid for civil war. On one side, the rebels had secured the support of roughly half Spain's **Peninsular** army in addition to the Army of Africa, supplying them with around ninety-six thousand troops. On the other, the government had been left with less than half the national supply of rifles, heavy and light machine guns, and artillery pieces. Officer defections had severely weakened all Republican units. Both sides had a small collection of tanks, naval vessels, and outdated aircraft.

Coup Opposers

Grouped uncomfortably under the banner of the Popular Front, opposition to the coup was largely from those on the left of the political divide. However, there were still strong ideological differences between the factions and these would later cause debilitating tensions within the forces. The group was composed of Communists, socialists, liberals, and Catalans, with additional support from the Basque people and anarchists. Every section brought their own support base and complications.

The Communists were very influential within the Popular Front. This was in large part due to their support from the USSR, which quickly became one of the Front's few financial supporters, providing funds and weapons—though only enough to prolong the conflict rather than finish it.

Socialists, led by Francisco Largo Caballero, also played a key role within the Popular Front. The Socialist Party (PSOE) was founded in Spain in 1879. It began life as a Marxist organization and remained a small party until World War I. Its main support bases were Madrid, the mining community of Asturias, and the industrial areas of Bilbao.

Largo Caballero had originally served in the Republican government of 1931 as minister of labor. He had advocated the distribution of land to landless laborers and increased support for the PSOE in rural communities. In 1936, he was appointed prime minister by President Azaña after the Popular Front defeated the ring-wing government at the general election. His policies quickly outraged the left as he introduced conscription, the reintroduction of ranks and insignia into the military, and the abolition of workers' and soldiers' councils. Many in the Communist Party were highly critical of him, and this tension would continue into the Spanish Civil War.

Liberals were largely the remains of the Republican Left Party, led by Manuel Azaña, and the Republican Union Party. The Union party was formed and led by Diego Martinez Barrio. It was Martinez Barrio who assisted Azaña in establishing the coalition that would become the Popular Front. He was also a firm believer in the Front's platform policies, such as Catalan autonomy, amnesty for political prisoners, agrarian reform, and an end to political blacklists. Catalans were also major supporters of the Popular Front and fiercely opposed to the coup. This was primarily because of the Front's willingness to gain autonomy for the region of Catalonia.

The group also received some minor support from the Basque region and anarchists. The Basque support was slightly unusual, as the region had traditionally been conservative and deeply Catholic. However, as a territory wishing for its own autonomy, Basques probably believed this goal would be more easily accomplished with a Popular Front administration. Anarchists were also not completely convinced by the Popular

Front's politics. Rather than support the party against the Nationalist government, the Anarchist Party had originally instructed its supporters to boycott the 1936 election entirely. It was also one of the most powerful left-wing parties with very strong support in the poor south, more so than their Communist or socialist counterparts. However, they would later fight alongside the Popular Front against Nationalists.

Supporters of the Coup

The National Front similarly brought together a number of different political factions; yet these groups had the advantage of being much more politically close. These included the CEDA Party, monarchists, Carlists, the Radical Party, and the Falange Party. These parties had been particularly angered by the Popular Front's measures to transfer right-wing military leaders such as Francisco Franco to foreign posts, outlaw the Falange Party, and grant political and administrative autonomy to Catalonia.

CEDA was established in 1933 by José Maria Gil Robles from a number of smaller right-wing parties opposed to Manuel Azaña's Republican government. In that year's election, CEDA had won the majority of the Cortes' seats. However, just three years later, the right-wing government was ousted by the Popular Front. Most of the CEDA's members fully supported the Nationalist Army during the civil war. CEDA was the largest political party in Spain at the time the conflict broke.

The Carlists supported the coup and wanted to see a return to monarchy.

Many monarchists were also attracted to the National Front's cause. As fervent supporters of the monarchy, they were outraged by Spain's dissolution of the royal house and wished the institution to be reinstated—a belief held by many Nationalists. Similarly to monarchists, Carlists were extremely conservative and Catholic. They too wanted to restore the monarchy; however, they supported a rival claimant. After the **deposition** of Alfonso XIII, the Carlists were at the forefront of opposition to the second republic. Strongly opposed to liberal secularism and political or economic modernization, they received considerable support from the Catholic Church and held strong bases in Navarre, Valencia, Aragon, and Old Castile. By 1936, the Carlist Youth had thirty thousand members, of which an estimated third were armed, making them the strongest right-wing paramilitary force in Spain.

The right-wing middle classes were represented by the Radical Party, also known as the Radical Republican Party. Founded in 1908 by Alejandro Lerroux, the group was formed after a dramatic split from the Republican Union Party. Somewhat surprisingly, they supported not only republicanism but also social liberalism, anticlericalism, and were opposed to the autonomization of Catalonia. They became involved with the right wing after the 1933 election when the party formed a rather weak government and eventually secured the support of the CEDA and later other conservatives.

Finally, the Falange Party completed the Nationalist Front. Initially a tiny Fascist organization, it grew in power and popularity dramatically after the 1936 election. Falange Española was first established in October 1933 and in its manifesto, the Falangists condemned socialism, Marxism, republicanism, and capitalism. They went as far as to argue that Spain should become a Fascist state mirroring Benito Mussolini's regime in Italy. In the 1936 election, the fringe party took just 0.7 percent of the vote. However, upon the establishment to the Popular Front government, their membership grew rapidly, reaching over forty thousand by July of the same year. Upon the outbreak of war, the movement quickly became the dominant political force of the Nationalists. Later, when Franco became Spain's principal political leader, he had little difficulty uniting the Falange with the Carlists and smaller right-wing group to form the Falange Española Tradicionalista.

Foreign Influencers

Though the civil war began as a purely Spanish conflict, it soon pulled other countries into its orbit. In many ways, it mirrored the political disputes playing out across Europe as Fascism, democracy, and Communism fought for ideological control. Some historians have even compared the Spanish conflict to a dress rehearsal for World War II.

As resources and morale dwindled, foreign aid and support became increasingly important. Propaganda held a key position in the fight. Nationalists were determined to represent themselves as the cause of Christian order and Western civilization against Communism. The Republicans, on the other hand, focused on the legal argument that they were the elected government and under threat from Fascism and dictatorship.

The Nationalists were supported by Fascist powers Italy and Germany, with both countries sending aid. Germany provided roughly sixteen thousand men, two hundred tanks, and six hundred planes. German tactics would later become infamous for their targeting of civilians, one particular

German troops gave the Nationalists a key advantage. Here, the German Condor Legion parades after returning home from the war.

example being the bombing of Guernica. The Nazi German Luftwaffe's Condor Legion carried out such actions on the orders of the Spanish Nationalist government. German planes gave the Nationalists the air superiority that would be crucial to victory. One benefit the Germans received from this deal was the ability to use Spain as a testing ground for their new military technology, and also for the development of **blitzkrieg** tactics. Italy similarly contributed a number of resources, including seventy-five thousand troops, one hundred and fifty tanks, and six hundred and sixty aircraft. Historians have often cited the Italian contribution as being of particular value, as it was not only enormous but also more generalized than the German.

Spanish Nationalists also received aid from other countries. Among them were twelve thousand troops from Portugal and seven hundred volunteers from Ireland.

Most democratic countries within Europe followed a policy of nonintervention, choosing to remain neutral instead. Britain and France were at the forefront of this resolution and tried in vain to prevent foreign aid from being sent to either side in order to speed up the conflict's completion. The United States also remained neutral. This decision was largely prompted by the powerful American-Catholic lobby. As a result, the Republicans struggled to purchase arms from abroad. This severely hampered their resistance efforts. Without European support, the Republicans turned to the Soviet Union, hoping its Communist members would carry favor with their leader, Joseph Stalin. Russia sent the Republicans two thousand five hundred men, one thousand planes, and nine hundred tanks. Stalin's support was largely piecemeal and not reliable. His primary concern was keeping Germany occupied and away from Eastern Europe, and as such, the country only ever sent enough resources to prolong the conflict without necessarily securing victory.

International Brigades

The Republicans' key international resource was, in fact, the international brigades. These were volunteers from all over Europe and the United States who had come to support the fight against Fascism. To many, the Republicans were a beacon for freedom, democracy, and **enlightenment**, and Nationalist massacres and bombings were used as evidence that international involvement was not only necessary but a moral requirement. The brigades were mainly composed of Communist volunteers from countries such as France, Britain, Ireland, and even Germany. In total, there were roughly fifty thousand men from fifty-three different countries.

Many of the battalions named themselves after famous revolutions or revolutionaries. The French were known as the Commune de Paris, and the Americans were the George Washington battalion. They used slogans, such as "No pasarán (They will not pass)" and "Spain—the graveyard of European Fascism."

Control of the brigades was allocated to the Communist movement, known as the Comintern, and they operated outside the command of the Republican army. These volunteers became known for their great courage and were often subjected to savage discipline—over five hundred were shot for political offences alone. They also became unknowingly embroiled in internal power struggles as Communists attempted to use the brigades against their political enemies, the socialists and anarchists. The brigades

Ernest Hemingway (center left) *was just one of a number of American and European writers who joined the Popular Front.*

were finally withdrawn in October 1938 when the position of the republic became seemingly hopeless.

Many writers and reporters traveled to Spain during the conflict to document the war or to join the brigades. Among the most famous were the novelists Ernest Hemingway, who worked as a journalist and photographer, and George Orwell, who joined the brigades.

One of the most interesting aspects of the Spanish Civil War is how history has remembered its events. Unlike the majority of conflicts, its narrative has been largely written not by its winners, but by its losers. The Nationalists' Italian and German support has led to vilification by association in the annals of history, while the Republicans were given the unanimous support of Europe's intellectuals due to the work of writers, painters, and poets who lived through or joined the conflict.

The Course of Conflict

1936

After the failure of the 1936 coup, the country was divided. Half of Spain's troops were still loyal to the government, and rebel forces had failed to take major centers such as Madrid, Valencia, Barcelona, and the Basque country. Militias of peasants and ordinary workers formed to defend their elected government; however, Spain's elite Army of Africa, led by General Franco, supported the coup.

By August, the rebels occupied most of northern and northwestern Spain, while the government held the south and the north coast. Both sides appealed for international aid, but only pro-Fascist countries responded. Italy and Germany sent over troops and equipment for the Nationalists, while Britain and France took an official stance of nonintervention. Only the Soviets responded to the Republican call. With the help of German transport planes, Franco's Army of Africa was moved from Morocco to Spain.

Nationalists now attempted to storm Madrid. Bloody battles ensued as the rebels tried to encircle and capture the city, but they were beaten back by Republicans. Finally, in November, the Nationalists called off the assault. After the temporary victory, Communist influence within Madrid grew. However, fear and suspicion increased in equal measure, and soon arrests and executions were taking place to purge the city of suspected Nationalists.

In September, Nationalist forces captured the city of Toledo and relieved a small garrison that had been under siege from Republicans since the end of July. In the same month, Largo Caballero, the socialist leader, became prime minister. The government moved to the safety of Valencia just two months later. Concerned over its poor stock of weaponry, the Republican government sent most of the country's gold reserves to Russia for military equipment. The sale of gold reserves caused a swift rise in inflation in Republican-held zones. Foreign volunteers arrived in the country, coinciding with the first shipment of weaponry from Russia, and were organized into the international brigades. By October, General Franco was appointed head of the Nationalist government of Spain.

1937

As the war moved into 1937, the Nationalists began offensives in February at Jarama and Guadalajara. Both efforts were aimed at capturing Madrid for the rebels and were stopped by Republicans, but with heavy casualties. In March, the Nationalists began their attack of the Basque country with a horrific bombing of the town of Guernica in April by Germany's Condor Legion. Basque morale collapsed and by June the capital, Bilbao, had fallen to the rebels. The profits and resources of the Basque country's industry were now under Nationalist control.

In the same month, Franco merged the Carlist, Falange, and other right-wing factions into a single party known as the Nationalist Movement. Their unity, in contrast to the

THE BATTLE OF BADAJOZ

The Battle of Badajoz on August 14, 1936, was one of the first Nationalist victories in the Spanish Civil War. The capture of the city effectively meant that the Spanish republic was henceforth cut off from its neighbor Portugal. The victory also connected the northern and southern zones of Nationalist control.

That summer, German and Italian air support had transported almost ten thousand Spanish troops across the Straits of Gibraltar to southern Spain. Nationalist forces, led by Franco, assembled at Seville. On August 1, Franco and his troops departed northward to join General Mola's forces.

Three days prior to the full attack, Badajoz had experienced a continual bombardment from Nationalist artillery. The city was flooded with refugees and its populace was grim and anxious.

On the morning of August 14, the Nationalists launched their full attack, storming the Trinity Gate with a unit of the Spanish Foreign Legion. This assault was checked by the determined resistance of Republican machine guns. However, the Nationalists ignored these losses and pressed on with armored cars. Eventually the gate was won and fighters poured into the breach. Hand-to-hand combat filled the streets. On the south side of the city, the walls fell to the onslaught of Nationalist units.

Many of the loyalist soldiers defected to the Nationalist side and gave easier access to the city for the attackers. Street fighting raged until nightfall. The Republican colonel Ildefonso Puigengolas, the city major, and other members of the defense committee slipped out of the city the following morning and fled to Portugal. In the aftermath, the Republicans suffered losses of 750 soldiers and a further 3,500 were wounded or captured.

Republicans' numerous divisions, would prove to be a decisive factor in the outcome of the war.

By May, the Republicans' lack of cohesion had begun to cause huge tensions and led to fatal errors. For instance, in Barcelona, internal conflicts resulted in violence. Socialists and Communists were embroiled in street warfare with anarchists and Trotskyites. When the latter finally prevailed, a bloody purge of the ranks was carried out against the perceived enemies of Communism. Republican prime minister Cabarello hesitated over whether to send in troops, fearing it might violate Catalan autonomy. On the morning of May 6, hit squads invaded the homes of numerous well-known anarchists and assassinated them. The situation had reached critical mass, and the following day, Republican troops were finally sent in to retake control of Barcelona. It is believed that more than four hundred people died in the May riots. The event severely damaged popular support for the Republicans and as a result, Caballero was replaced by Juan Negrin, a Communist sympathizer.

With this action, the Soviet Union's Joseph Stalin gained further control over the policies of the Republican government, and the role of Communist members expanded exponentially in all government-controlled areas of Spain. This reorganization spilled over into their media as well with the use of inspiring speeches from Dolores Ibárruri, chief propagandist for the republic, to raise morale. Yet the continued brutal use of secret police, known as the SIM, and their intolerance of all and any opposition led to a reversal in public opinion, with many wondering if life would not be

Fierce fighting was seen in Spain's streets and civilians were often caught in the crossfire. Here, a civilian in Teruel is ferried to safety.

better under Franco. Attempts by Republicans to prevent the capture of Madrid led to an inconclusive battle at Brunete. In the closing month of 1937, the Republicans saw the defeat of their offensive at Teruel after prolonged and bitter fighting.

1938

After Nationalist forces captured the key city of Teruel, the rebels continued pushing forward across the country; by April they had reached the Mediterranean, effectively splitting Republican-held Spain and isolating Catalonia from Popular Front support. July saw a new Republican offensive launched by General Modesto at the Ebro River. Despite some early successes, the offensive ultimately ended in November with the defeat of government forces. In December, the Nationalists began their advance into Catalonia.

1939

Within the first three months of 1939, the republic began to collapse. In January, Nationalist forces finally took control

The Battle of Toledo
(July 21 to September 27, 1936)

Also known as the Siege of the Alcázar, the battle was fought in the early stages of the war. It was held by pro-Nationalist forces after the Nationalist uprising. Militias connected to the Popular Front laid siege to win back control, but they ultimately lost after the arrival of the Army of Africa under the command of Franco.

The Battle of Jarama
(February 6 to 27, 1937)

An indecisive battle where Nationalist forces attempted to dislodge Republican lines along the Jarama River, east of Madrid. Legionnaires and regulars of the Army of Africa battled the Republican army and international brigades, but after days of fierce combat no clear victory was achieved. Both sides took heavy casualties.

The Battle of Guadalajara
(March 8 to 23, 1937)

A key Republican victory where the People's Republican Army defeated Italian and Nationalist forces attempting to encircle Madrid. After a series of halted Italian offences, the Republican troops launched a successful counterattack between March 18 and 23. The strategic victory did much to raise Republican morale. Italy received ridicule from the international community, and morale amongst Italian volunteers experienced a heavy blow.

The Battle of Madrid
(November 8, 1936 to March 28, 1939)

The Battle of Madrid was a two-and-a-half-year siege of the Spanish capital followed by intense fighting in and around the city. The Republicans initially repulsed the Nationalist assault in 1936, but eventually the capital fell to Franco.

of Barcelona, and by March they had captured Madrid. This essentially marked the end of the war, and Franco made an official declaration to this effect on April 1.

In the course of the conflict, roughly half a million people were killed, with hundreds of thousands dying in atrocities committed on both sides. The largest number of deaths was caused by Nationalist troops as they took control of government areas. Their tactics were often ruthless. For instance, when the city of Badajoz was captured in August 1936, over one thousand five hundred of its citizens were shot in batches, in the town's bullring, for defending their homes. It is estimated that around two hundred thousand people were executed by Nationalists during the war.

Republicans, though, were equally capable of bloody and cruel actions. Their violence was often more spontaneous, usually not official policy of the Republican administration, and largely aimed against landowners, businessmen, the police, and the Catholic Church. They were responsible for roughly twenty thousand deaths, though many of those were the result of Communist purges of their political enemies, such as anarchists in Barcelona and Madrid. After the fall of the Republican government, half a million refugees fled to France. Some were handed back to Franco during World War II after Nazi forces captured France in 1940.

Franco's Victory

Franco's success was built on a number of factors, both internal and international, and it was as a result of these that Fascism won Spain's ideological war. General Francisco Franco was not considered a man of either vision or energy; however, he has been widely acknowledged as an excellent field commander. His tactics of cautious and gradual progress allowed the Nationalists to claw back power even after their failed coup in 1936.

In addition to this, Franco held a number of influential power bases. He had the support of the army, capitalists, landowners, and the Catholic Church—and he was well resourced. Hitler provided him with sixteen thousand German troops and the Condor Air Legion, and Mussolini supplied seventy-five thousand Italian soldiers. These forces massively outweighed foreign support for Republicans.

Britain and French neutrality further tipped the scales in favor of the Nationalists. The arms embargo spearheaded by the two countries only ensured that Republicans would not receive international aid; however, most countries turned a blind eye to supporters of Franco. Fascist support was also much better organized than Republican support. German and Italian resources were delivered on time and directly channeled through Franco, while Soviet supplies for the Republicans were often late and only able to cover the bare minimum requirement. As previously mentioned, Russian aid was intended merely to prolong the conflict; Italian and German support was designed to win it. Lastly, while the Popular Front was ultimately irreconcilably divided in their ideology, Franco managed to hold together his National Front and ensure the various right-wing groups worked together to achieve a common goal.

3

Changing
Ideas

War does not exist within a vacuum. Many things can be caught up by and influenced by the course of conflict—not just people and places but art, philosophy, and technology. War can sometimes slow and entirely destroy culture, but often it can also shape its next evolution. Such a provoking subject inevitably draws out new ideas and concepts that simultaneously respond to and impact the surrounding society. The Spanish Civil War forever changed the face of Spain, but it also deeply affected a number of other factors in both Spanish and European life. Three key impacts the conflict had were on the perception and spread of Communism, the career of Pablo Picasso, and the use of art and propaganda to create narratives around warfare.

Opposite: *The 1937 World's Fair in Paris put a spotlight on the Spanish conflict through art.*

The Spread of Communism

Communism is defined in the *Oxford English Dictionary* as "A theory or system of social organization in which all property is owned by the community and each person contributes and receives according to their ability and needs." It operates on the principles of a society built on common ownership of the means of production and the absence of social classes, money, and the state itself. The political philosophy combines a variety of schools of thought, including Marxism, a socioeconomic method of analysis of class relations and societal conflict, and anarchism, the belief in the abolition of all government and the creation of a society run on a voluntary, cooperative basis.

The exact origins of Communism are still debated by historians, but in its modern recognized form it is largely agreed to have been the **brainchild** of Karl Marx and Friedrich Engels. Marx was a German-born writer and philosopher, and Engels was a German social scientist and journalist. Together the pair wrote *The Communist Manifesto*, published in 1848, which put forth the idea of a cooperative, people-led society and argued against the idea of capitalism as the optimal economic system.

The first recognized Communist society began in 1917 after the October Revolution in Russia. This action set the conditions for Lenin's Bolsheviks to rise to power—the first time any acknowledged Communist party had reached that position.

Communism in Spain and Reactions Abroad

The first avowedly Communist party in Spain was established on April 15, 1920. Known as the *Partido Comunista Español* (Spanish Communist Party), the organization formed from members of the Federation of Socialist Youth, the Spanish branch of an international political youth organization. Soon after, on November 14, 1921, the party merged yet again with the *Partido Comunista Obrero Español* (Spanish Communist Workers' Party) to form the *Partido Comunista de España* (Communist Party of Spain, or PCE). By the end of 1922, the PCE had over five thousand members. Its left wing was heavily involved in political violence, mainly concentrated in the Bilbao area and mostly directed at other leftists. This aggression toward other leftist factions would reemerge during the Spanish Civil War, causing fatal unity issues. When Miguel Primo de Rivera became dictator in 1923, political parties, including the PCE, were repressed and rendered almost powerless, though they were not dissolved.

During the first years of the second Spanish republic, the PCE was a relatively small party until the victory of the Popular Front and the beginning of the civil war. PCE members worked consistently for a Republican victory during the war, but at the same time the party was suspicious of what it saw as a government revolution being waged against Spanish workers. A major factor of the group's effectiveness was its close-knit and well-disciplined nature, especially in comparison to the Popular Front's other factions. In just the first five months of the conflict, its membership grew from thirty thousand to one hundred thousand. The PCE was also responsible for founding a Spanish branch of the International Red Aid, which assisted the Republican side considerably.

In the wider world, Communism was viewed with deep suspicion by most European governments, as well as the American government. It was perceived as a rival of and threat to not only capitalism but to Christianity. It was these two factors in particular that cemented Britain and France's resistance to helping the Republicans, while in the United States, the powerful Catholic lobby used its significant influence to block shipments of weaponry and financial aid to the Popular Front troops.

Anti-Communist Sentiments in Spain

Communism and anticlericalism were often seen as inseparable. The vast majority of Spanish Communists wanted to completely eradicate or at least severely curb the power of the Catholic Church. This sentiment was echoed among many of the other leftist factions of the Popular Front. So outspoken was their dislike of the Catholic Church that it quickly led to widespread fear among right-wing citizens and moderates that the republic was attempting to bring about a Bolshevik revolution. One historian, Michael Alpert, described the situation as follows: "For Spanish Catholics the battle was between stark alternatives: godless Bolshevism on the one side, Eternal Spain and the Church on the other."

EDWARD KNOBLAUGH

American journalist Edward Knoblaugh worked for the Associated Press in Madrid just before the violence broke out in 1936. While living in Spain, he interviewed many leading politicians connected to the conflict.

After returning to the United States, he published an account of his time there. In one key section, he described the first siege of Madrid and Franco's tactics. Twenty-five thousand volunteers had arrived from training in Albacete, along with large quantities of guns and ammunition. Franco had managed to enter the city, but his troops could proceed no further. The volunteers worked to construct fortifications, and the city's demoralized militia had regrouped and were now helping the international brigade. Knoblaugh explained how difficult it was:

> Military men know how difficult it is to capture a large city which has been converted into a veritable fortress, unless that city can be completely surrounded and its communications cut. Franco took Malago and Bilbao and other cities by pincering them in this fashion. Madrid was a more difficult problem.

The main issue for Franco was Madrid's size—its circumference almost 32 miles (51.5 kilometers) wide. This made huge troop numbers extremely important. However, Franco did not have such numbers available at this early point of the war. Knoblaugh estimated that Franco had no more than forty thousand men for the assault on Madrid.

The defending Republicans also had another advantage. Their position and holding of a city prized by Franco granted certain benefits. Knoblaugh explained that Franco did not want to completely destroy Madrid, which would become his capital city, because it would mean harming his own supporters. There were indeed Nationalists living within the city. In addition, there were also a large number of properties owned by the very men who were financing his campaign.

Pablo Picasso circa 1937

In the years leading to the civil war, fear and resentment had built to such a fever pitch that by 1936 Catholic right-wingers were beginning to justify armed rebellion.

Picasso's Masterpiece

World War I encouraged the mass migration of many artists, writers, and creatives. Some were escaping repressive regimes, and some were looking for a more liberal and progressive environment. Many found their way to Paris, France, as a result of the city's culture, history, and artistic schools. One such artist was Pablo Picasso.

The Spanish artist Pablo Ruiz y Picasso, better known as Pablo Picasso, was born October 25, 1881, to Don José Ruiz y Blasco and María Picasso y López. The son of a painter himself, Picasso would eventually become one of the most famous and influential artists of the twentieth century. He was baptized a Catholic before later becoming an atheist. At the time of the civil war, Picasso was living in Paris, France. He had last visited Spain in 1934 and would never return to his native homeland.

Despite his lack of firsthand experience, it was the Spanish Civil War and one of its most notorious massacres that would be the basis of his masterpiece, *Guernica*.

On April 26, 1937, the Nazi Luftwaffe's Condor Legion and the Fascist Italian Aviazione Legionaria launched an aerial bombing of the Basque town of Guernica, under the codename "Operation Rügen" and at the request of the Spanish Nationalist government. It caused horror throughout Europe due to its deliberate targeting of civilians. The number of victims is still disputed to this day, with figures ranging from four hundred to over one thousand five hundred deaths.

Guernica was the title of a mural-sized oil painting on canvas. Completed in 1937, it depicted in Picasso's signature style the bombing of Guernica. Standing at 11 feet 6 inches (3.49 meters) high and 25 feet 6 inches (7.76 m) wide, the painting used a somber palette of gray, white, and black to depict the suffering of Guernica's citizens in a modern symbolic fashion. Picasso took inspiration from the Italian master Leonardo da Vinci's *The Battle of Anghiari*. While he was influenced by the work's energy and immediacy,

Picasso's Guernica *would become the defining image of the Spanish Civil War.*

he spurned its classical technique for a more avant-garde narrative artwork. Through the use of shadows and light, symbolically Spanish characters, and abstract contorted shapes, Picasso captured the grief, horror, and fear of the attack and the suffering of the Spanish people. He used symbols such as a wounded bull, a traditional symbol of Spain, to link the work directly to the conflict. In the end, *Guernica* captured the fractured and mutilated spirit of Spain, and the sense of agony and desperation that had overtaken the country.

The work was not simply an artistic whim, however, but a government commission. In January 1937, the Spanish Republican government requested Picasso create a large mural to be displayed at the Exposition Internationale des Arts et Techniques dans la Vie Moderne, as part of the 1937 World's Fair in Paris. Picasso was already living in Paris by this time and had been named honorary director-in-exile of the Prado Museum. He was initially less than enthused and worked on some preliminary sketches involving his studio until late April, but without much passion.

On April 26, reports came through of the bombing of Guernica. The Spanish poet and essayist Juan Larrea visited Picasso to urge him to use Guernica as the subject of his painting. However, it was not until May 1 and the publication of the British journalist George Steer's eyewitness account that things began to move. What Picasso read in Steer's article caused him to abandon his original project and begin a new series of sketches that would eventually become *Guernica*.

In order to raise awareness for the anti-Fascist cause, Picasso allowed visitors into his studio to observe the painting's progress. Up until this moment, he had rarely allowed any strangers into his studio. During the painting of the mural, Picasso explained:

> *The Spanish struggle is the fight of reaction against the people, against freedom. My whole life as an artist has been nothing more than a continuous struggle against reaction and the death of art. How could anybody think for a moment that I could be in agreement with reaction and death? ... In the panel on which I am working, which I shall call Guernica, and in all my recent works of art, I clearly express my abhorrence of the military caste which has sunk Spain in an ocean of pain and death.*

He finished the painting on June 4, 1937, after thirty-five days of work. Once completed, the painting was exhibited in the Spanish section of the Exposition Internationale des Arts et Techniques dans la Vie Moderne, also known as the Paris International Exposition, at the 1937 World's Fair. It would later tour and be displayed in many locations alongside other Republican masterpieces. The piece's large size grabbed the public's attention, casting a much-needed spotlight on the mounting horror of Spain's civil war, and its later touring exhibition was used to raise funds for the Spanish war relief. The painting was widely acclaimed and considered a great success for both Picasso and the Republican cause.

After *Guernica*, Picasso remained in Paris. He continued to stay even during the German occupation of the city. However, his style did not suit or conform to the Nazi ideal, so Picasso did not exhibit during this period. In addition, he was frequently harassed by the Gestapo, the secret police of both Nazi Germany and German-occupied Europe. During one such raid on his Paris apartment, an officer saw a photograph of the *Guernica* painting and asked, "Did you do that?" Picasso responded: "No. You did."

Guernica is now internationally recognized as one of the greatest antiwar paintings ever, due to its moving and striking depictions. It remains a powerful symbol in the twenty-first century.

Art and Propaganda

Propaganda is an often-misunderstood genre of communication. We believe it is something inherently dishonest and used by **totalitarian** governments to lie to or oppress its own people. However, propaganda is fundamentally a tool, sometimes for negative ends, but more often used as a means to maintain morale and courage amongst a populace in wartime. In the Spanish Civil War, both sides frequently used propaganda. Motion pictures, posters, books, radio, and leaflets were all used both at home and abroad.

At home, information was delivered to inspire the masses and aid recruitment to the war effort. Abroad, propaganda was distributed to encourage international concern for the Spanish people, to request military or financial aid, or shape the narrative the conflict was creating on the world's stage.

Nationalist propaganda was largely built and played on an international fear of Communism. They devised a media campaign where Nationalists were represented as the cause of "Christianity, order and Western civilization against 'Asiatic Communism.'" They intentionally exacerbated fears and justified their own actions by alleging that Communists in Spain had planned a revolution with one hundred fifty thousand **shock troops** and one hundred thousand reserves for 1936, a move that had been preempted by the Nationalist uprising.

Many foreign journalists traveled to the battle sites of Spain to interview Popular Front fighters.

Despite the fact that Nationalist organizations had previously accepted the results of the 1936 election, which brought the Popular Front to power, Nationalists now claimed the results were invalid. In all Nationalist media, life in Republican zones was portrayed as a "perpetual massacre of priests, nuns and innocents, accompanied by a frenzied destruction of churches and works of art." And to justify their failure to take Madrid, they claimed that half a million foreign Communists were fighting in Spain. The Nationalists' key policy was to focus on small, powerful lobbies in Britain and the United States, unlike the wider and more engrossing efforts of the Republicans. However, these more selective movements proved to be incredibly effective. The fear of Communism combined with appeals to conservative and religious feeling, and an emphasis on the military aid the Republicans were receiving from the Soviet Union, ensured that those countries that did not side with the Nationalists would at the very least not assist the Republicans.

Republican propaganda in many ways had a number of advantages the Nationalists lacked. As the more liberal of the two causes, Republicans drew some of the twentieth century's greatest artists to their banner. Their liberalization also extended to a huge amount of freedom granted to writers and photographers when documenting battles, something that Nationalists severely restricted their own reporters from doing. However, the Republicans also began with a negative image they needed to dispel to win support. Their Communist base was held responsible for a series of "red massacres" at the conflict's start. As a result of this, many Western governments refused aid to the Republicans, and thus the courting of writers and journalists soon became essential. In addition to the use of posters and radio recruitment drives, Soviet films were also highly effective in spreading Republican ideals and boosting morale.

The War's Influence on Writers and Artists

The conflict did not only leave a lasting impact on Spain's landscape and people, but also on European art. A large number of books, films, and artwork were produced during the late 1930s, and the conflict continues to inspire creatives around the world today. Ernest Hemingway and several other famous early-twentieth-century writers coproduced a film to raise awareness of the conflict and encourage military and monetary aid. The work was named *The Spanish Earth* and premiered in America in July 1937. The following year, the British author George Orwell wrote a personal account of his experiences fighting in the international brigades, entitled *Homage to Catalonia*. Orwell served as a private, then a corporal, and finally a lieutenant in both Catalonia and Aragon. He was initially tied to the militia of the Workers' Party of Marxist Unification. However, this organization was firmly anti-Stalin and after it was declared illegal, Orwell was forced to flee or face imprisonment.

In addition to film and literature, the conflict inspired artists around the world. Although Picasso and *Guernica* are perhaps the most famous artist and piece associated with the era, many sculptures were also created. Paris in particular had become a haven for artists in the aftermath of World War I. It seemed to hold a promise of exhibitions, commissions, and even fame. Many Spanish artists had moved to Paris to chase that dream and some of them would later have their work displayed in the Spanish pavilion at the 1937 World's Fair in Paris.

Alberto Sánchez Pérez designed a 41-foot- (12.5 m) high plaster monolith representing the struggle for a socialist utopia. He named it *El pueblo español tiene un camino que conduce a una estrella maqueta* or "The Spanish people have a path that leads to a star."

Antiwar works were equally popular. In 1935, one year before the conflict's start, the Spanish artist Julio González created *La Montserrat* from a sheet of iron. The material had been hammered and welded into the shape of a peasant mother carrying a small child in one arm and a sickle in the other. It was intended as a symbol of both Catalonia and motherhood. González had been taught how to work with metal from an early age and pioneered welding techniques in sculpture. He was known for his pessimistic views on warfare and said of his sculpture:

It is high time that this metal ceases to be a murderer and the simple instrument of an overly mechanical

science. Today, the door is opened wide for this material to be—at last!—forged and hammered by the peaceful hands of artists.

"

Spanish artist Joan Miró completed his painting *El segador*, or *The Reaper*, just two years later, building upon the same themes but now in the context of civil war. The large mural, spanning 18 feet by 12 feet (5.5 m by 3.7 m), showed a Catalan peasant holding a sickle. When asked about his work's political message, he responded:

"

Of course I intended it as a protest … The Catalan peasant is a symbol of the strong, the independent, the resistant. The sickle is not a communist symbol. It is the reaper's symbol, the tool of his work, and, when his freedom is threatened, his weapon.

"

Sadly, the work went missing or was destroyed in 1938, and only a few black and white photographs remain.

Another famous protest work, entitled *Fuente de mercurio*, or *Mercury fountain*, was completed in 1937 by the American artist Alexander Calder. Similarly to González's *La Montserrat*, it was displayed alongside *Guernica* at that year's World's Fair. It was dedicated as a memorial to the siege of Almadén by Nationalist troops, a location which then supplied 60 percent of world's mercury.

The impact of these artists and their contribution to the Spanish pavilion at the 1937 World's Fair is not to be underestimated. As the historian Anthony Beevor argued:

66

In the spring of 1937, when the republicans were at last starting to win the propaganda war, the International Exhibition of Arts took place in Paris. The Republic's pavilion became famous with the display of Picasso's Guernica, *but also the work of many other great artists, including Joan Miró, Alexander Calder, Luis Lacasa, Josep Lluís Sert, Horacio Ferrer and Antoni Bonet. The nationalist government put on its own exhibition, but it had to be under the Vatican flag.*

99

The Republicans were creating a narrative through art that would affect history's view of the entire conflict. Though they were not victorious, generations have identified Republicans as noble freedom fighters and firmly placed Nationalists as the enemies of liberalism and progress, primarily due to the legacy created through pro-Republican books, films, and art.

THE FIFTEENTH INTERNATIONAL BRIGADE

The Fifteenth International Brigade was a mixed outfit of English-speaking volunteers fighting for the Spanish republic during the Spanish Civil War. They received the nickname *Brigada Abraham Lincoln*, or the Abraham Lincoln Brigade, as many of their regiment were from the United States. It was common for international brigades to be named after famous figures from their individual countries. The Fifteenth was composed of four battalions: British, North American, the Balkan "Dimitrov", and the Franco-Belgian "Sixth February."

The brigade fought at Jarama, the Ebro River, Brunete, Tueruel, Boadilla, Fuentes de Ebro, and Belchite. Their members included Theodore Cogswell, an American science-fiction author, and Ralph Fasanella, an Italian-American painter who later rose to fame for his depictions of urban working life and his critiques of post–World War II America.

The fighters and their actions inspired writers and singers in future generations. One of the most famous examples is contemporary Irish folk singer Christy Moore's song "Viva La Quinta Brigada." Inspired by a Spanish war song and the autobiography of civil war veteran Michael O'Riordan, the song tells the story of a small contingent of Irish volunteers within the Fifteenth International Brigade. Its lyrics emphasize the bond of brotherhood between the volunteers and praise their bravery in romanticized heroic language.

Aftermath

The year 1939 saw the end of one of the bloodiest conflicts in Spanish history and many of its military issues mirrored those experienced in World War I. Defense continued to be much easier than attack. During assaults on the city of Madrid, casualties were high and attackers were only ever able to take small amounts of ground. However, it was also a unique time where advancements in land warfare were first tried and tested, such as the German blitzkrieg where tanks, artillery, and air bombardment were used in order to prepare for a troop advance.

As the Republicans began to falter and fall under the weight of their own internal divisions, the Nationalists only grew in strength and fervor. Franco was ruthless in his wish to see a definite end to civil war and a complete victory for Fascism. Soon Europe too was forced to acknowledge that

Opposite: Urban battles left many Spanish towns and cities in ruins.

Franco's was in fact the true government of Spain. However, even as the fighting drew to a close, the scars left on the Spanish landscape and on its people were only just beginning to come to light. The wider world would not know the full extent of them for many years to come. Even today, decades after the end of Franco's regime in 1975, new evidence is emerging and historians continue to exhume hidden mass graves scattered throughout Spain.

Entering the Final Year

As the conflict entered 1939, its violence had escalated to new heights. Under the burden of huge losses, the Republican government became increasingly susceptible to corruption and further political division. Public support and internal organization decreased with each new Nationalist victory. Unlike the clumsy governance of the Republican officials, Nationalist leaders were ruthlessly effective at waging civil war and consistently clear about its ideology.

By this time, the Republican government, now under the leadership of Largo Caballero, was fractured by internal arguments and confused by its identity and beliefs. As Caballero's government slipped into further chaos, many Republicans began to question the point of further fighting. Morale sank dramatically throughout the Republican forces, yet it remained steadfastly high in the Nationalists' ranks. The bombing of Guernica in April 1937 had fatally wounded the Republican spirit. It convinced many across the country that to resist the Nationalists would result in another bloodbath. Soon the Republicans would be entirely morally crushed.

Franco's Victory

In the first two months of 1939, Franco's success was at an all-time high. His troops conquered Catalonia in a lightning-fast campaign. First Tarragona fell on January 15, then Barcelona was conquered on January 26, and finally Girona was taken on February 2. Once the Fascist forces had taken Barcelona they had unlimited access to French borders, causing concern throughout Europe. Catalonia finally collapsed during February, followed by Valencia and Madrid by the end of March.

Reluctant International Recognition

Despite Britain's nonintervention stance, not all of its politicians remained silent. Winston Churchill, the future UK prime minister, was extremely vocal in his concern over the effects of the Spanish Civil War. He was known for his hatred of Communism; however, he recognized the threat that a Fascist Spain would pose to Europe, especially in the case of a future war. He had paid careful attention to Hitler's involvement in the conflict and was deeply troubled by the fledgling political friendship between Germany and Italy. He perceived the Spanish Civil War and other conflicts happening in Abyssinia and Rhineland not as regional struggles but rather involving "the whole structure of Europe, with possibilities of realignment carrying the promise of deadly danger to England." However, by mid-February 1939, the Republican strongholds of Catalonia and Barcelona had fallen and Churchill was unable to rouse support in parliament to aid them. On February 27, 1939, Britain recognized Franco as the legitimate ruler of Spain.

After this, only Madrid and a select few cities were left still holding out against Nationalist forces. The Republican government was demoralized and internally confused. On March 5, the Republican army, led by Colonel Segismundo Casado and the politician Julián Besteiro, revolted against the prime minister, Juan Negrín. They immediately formed the Consejo Nacional de Defensa (National Defence Council), also known as the CND, in order to negotiate peaceful terms for an end to the conflict. Negrín fled to France the next day.

Certain members of the Republican army were violently **incensed** by what they saw as Casado and Besteiro's betrayal of the cause. Communist troops around Madrid quickly rose up against Casado's forces, creating a brief civil war within the civil war. Soon, though, the rebels were defeated and peace negotiations began between the CND and the Nationalists. Yet this was not satisfactory for Franco. Ruthlessly meticulous even in victory, Franco refused to accept anything less than an unconditional surrender. On March 26, Nationalist forces began an offensive on Madrid, which succeeded just two days later. By the final days of March, they controlled all Spanish territory.

Franco's victory speech hailed the end of the war, but not the persecution of Republican supporters.

Franco announced his victory in a radio speech on April 1, upon the surrender of the last Republican troops. In his final radio communication of the Spanish Civil War, Franco declared: "Today, after having disarmed and captured the Red Army, the Nationalist troops have secured their final military objective. The war is ended. Burgos, April 1, 1939. Year of Victory."

The Dust Settles: Spain in the Aftermath

Though the war's official end had now been marked in history, the suffering of its people was far from over. Franco emerged as Spain's dictator, but his victory had been purchased at great cost. Major cities had been destroyed, and Spain's population severely decreased as a result of military fighting, executions,

WINSTON CHURCHILL

Churchill had long been an admirer of Spain and Spanish society. He considered the country to be "one of the oldest branches in the tree of European nations." He also had personal connections to the country. His ancestor, John Churchill, first duke of Marlborough, made his fortune in the War of Spanish Succession (1701–1714). He was related to one of Spain's best-known and most enduring hereditary titles, the House of Alba, and friends with King Alfonso XIII himself.

The Nationalist uprising coincided with Churchill's "wilderness years," a period when he was out of government but remained extremely vocal on both national and international issues. He initially supported the military uprising, viewing the event through a distinctly anti-Communist lens and with a feeling of deep sympathy for the dethroned King Alfonso. In October 1936, he declared: "The hideous series of nightly butcheries have robbed the Madrid [Republican] government of the lineaments of civilized power." When meeting the Republican government's ambassador to London, Churchill was reported to have muttered, "Blood, blood, blood," and refused to shake the Spaniard's hand.

Later, once Hitler's ambitions became more evident, Churchill would repent and argue for Republican support as a way to block Germany's expansionist aims. He soon realized that Spanish Communists held less threat for Britain than a Fascist Spain allied to Hitler.

Churchill's ties with Spain continued after World War II through personal friendships, and in his final years he often visited the country as a private citizen.

and assassinations carried out by both sides. And there was more to come.

In his first decree as Spain's recognized dictator, Franco made clear what awaited those who had opposed the Nationalist Front: a campaign of terror designed to eradicate all political opposition. For the next forty years, democrats, liberals, socialists, Communists, and anarchists would be systematically targeted and terrorized by the Franquist regime. In the immediate aftermath of the conflict, thousands of Republicans were imprisoned and at least thirty thousand were executed. Depending on how the killings are calculated, these deaths range from fifty thousand to two hundred thousand. This period would be later renamed the "White Terror." Those not executed were forced into hard labor to build railroads, drain swamps, and dig canals. The vast majority of Spain's intellectuals fled abroad and the country lost a generation of teachers, lawyers, researchers, doctors, and famous writers, poets, artists, and musicians. Those intellectuals who stayed had to conform to Franco's ultra-conservative, Catholic, and authoritarian views.

Escape and Internment Camps

During the civil war and in the wake of Franco's ascension, hundreds of thousands of Republicans fled abroad. Roughly five hundred thousand people crossed into France alone. The French authorities tried to contain the refugees in internment

Thousands of Republicans were held in internment camps on the French border.

camps along the borders. These camps were often overcrowded and unsanitary. Examples include Camp Vernet, where twelve thousand Republicans were housed in squalid conditions.

In an effort to aid the migrants, the Chilean poet and politician Pablo Neruda, who was serving as consul in Paris at the time, organized 2,200 Republican exiles to immigrate to Chile abroad the ship SS *Winnipeg*. Those refugees who could not find relatives in France were encouraged to return to their home in Spain.

This was the case for the vast majority of refugees. The immigration policy had been made with the agreement of Franco's government, and as a result were immediately turned over to Nationalist authorities upon arrival in Irún. From there, the detainees were transferred to the Miranda de Ebro camp for what was known as "purification," according to the Law of Political Responsibilities. This decree was issued by Franco two months before the end of the war and was designed to target those loyal to the Republican administration. The law made supporters of the Republicans, both before and during the war, liable to punishment. This included the confiscation of land, large fines, or even death. Under these guidelines, the state acquired vast tracts of land from Republican supporters. The key objectives of the new Franquist regime were to restore power to the privileged class and control the working classes, and Spain's economy would suffer for it.

The state first cut wages and outlawed all political activism. The workers' unions of the CNT and the UGT were destroyed. Employment for any Republican who had escaped imprisonment became impossible. In rural areas, the harsh inequalities of the social and working system were maintained by the civil guard. The clerical reforms of the second Spanish republic were all repealed, and the Church was raised to a status it had not held since the eighteenth century. Historian Frances Lannon explains: "Government and church combined to preach order, hierarchy and discipline. The counterrevolution had triumphed." Similarly, the campaigns for Catalan and Basque autonomy ended. The use of Catalan, Basque, and Galician languages was forbidden and all power was centralized in Madrid.

Spaniards who had taken part in or supported the Nationalist coup were considered by the Franco regime to be of a superior race, and their victory proof that Republicans were of an inferior race. Children of Republicans were kidnapped in order to prevent "contamination and degeneration." These children would be **indoctrinated** into Franquist ideology and then given to reliable Nationalist Catholic couples to be "reeducated" against the views and actions of their own parents. Many children who had been evacuated abroad by their parents during the fighting were forced to return to Spain and were immediately made wards of the state, meaning that any parent in the newly Franquist Spain who attempted to send their child abroad would risk losing their child forever. The division and hatred created by such actions remained in Spanish society for decades to come.

Shortly after the official end of the conflict, the French government declared that the refugees were in fact political prisoners, and the French police attempted to round up those who had already been liberated from the camps. These people were then sent on to the Drancy internment camp before being deported to Nazi Germany. Roughly five thousand Spaniards died in the Mauthausen-Gusen concentration camp. This complex would later become one of the largest concentration camps in Germany during World War II and the last to be liberated by the Allies.

Unfinished Business

Even after Franco's declaration of victory, pockets of resistance continued fighting. The Spanish Maquis were a group of **guerrilla** fighters who continued to fight against the Nationalist regime into the early 1960s. They became known for their acts of sabotage, robberies to fund guerrilla activity, protests at the Spanish embassy in France, and assassinations of Francoists. This is in addition to their contributions fighting against Nazi Germany during World War II. However, the warfare was extremely irregular and was gradually reduced by military defeats and a lack of support from the demoralized populace.

Influence on World War II

From the start of the civil war, Hitler had made no secret of his support for a Nationalist regime. Publicly he justified this as a desire to prevent Communism from gaining a foothold in Western Europe. Privately, however, Hitler had more lucrative reasons for wanting a Fascist Spain. Germany was extremely interested in having the country as a trading partner, and in particular as a supplier of raw materials, such as iron ore. The possibility of Spain as a military ally was also an appealing one. Hitler believed that a "Fascist triangle" of Germany, Italy, and Spain would aid in surrounding and subduing France. The Spanish Civil War was simply one part of a larger Nazi policy aimed at distracting Britain and France from Hitler's activities in central and eastern Europe.

In additional to all this, the Spanish conflict allowed Nazi Germany to test Hitler's newly restored armed forces. He was particularly keen to assess the real-world performance of the Luftwaffe in combat. The troops provided to Franco would remain in Spain until victory was secured in April 1939.

After the attack of Guernica, foreign journalists found bomb casings bearing German markings. Once this was reported in the world press, there was international

Despite the similarities in their political beliefs, Franco and Hitler quickly developed a mutual dislike for one another.

condemnation of Nazi involvement in the Spanish war, and European governments became increasingly alert to Hitler's maneuvers.

Once German support was no longer needed, Hitler hoped to turn a newly victorious Franco into a pledged ally for any future German conflict. However, he soon found his help would not be reciprocated. After such a long and brutal period, Spain was in no position to offer financial or military aid. Hitler and Franco met in October 1940 and found that mutual dislike also prevented closer alliance. Franco demanded large amounts of food, military supplies, and foreign territory in return for committing Spain to another war. Hitler found his demands excessive, and the two leaders failed to reach any agreement. In the end, Spain agreed to remain neutral, with Franco allowing Nationalist volunteers to fight alongside Nazi forces against the Soviet Red Army. This small voluntary force was known as La División Azul.

Ramifications across Europe

Many have described the Spanish Civil War as a dress rehearsal for World War II. While this may be true in many ways, it was more accurately a determining factor. Its occurrence and consequences set the stage for further conflict and was also instrumental in drawing up its battle lines.

The war was a major contributor to deepening divisions between the democracies of Britain and France and the dictatorships of Italy and Germany. When Hitler and

THE CONDOR LEGION

Germany made large contributions to the Spanish Civil War and, in the process, expanded their own military capability. In September 1936, the German Lieutenant Colonel Walther Warlimont of the German General Staff was sent to Spain as the German commander and military advisor to General Francisco Franco. He immediately organized the formation of a German Condor Legion to be deployed by the Nationalists using German soldiers. Hitler had hoped that this measure would not be necessary, as Franco had claimed that he was close to victory. However, Franco's declaration was proved wrong, and by November, international brigades as well as resources from the Soviet Union had begun to arrive.

After Hitler had given consent for the Legion, an initial force was assembled. There were four key groups. The Bomber Group consisted of three squadrons for Ju-52 bombers. The Fighter Group was composed of three squadrons of He-51 fighters. The Reconnaissance Group was two squadrons of He-99 and He-70 reconnaissance bombers. Finally, the Seaplane Squadron was made up of He-59 and He-60 floatplanes.

The Condor Legion was commanded by General Hugo Sperrle and made an autonomous unit that would be responsive only to Franco. Its ranks comprised nearly twelve thousand men. The Legion participated in all major engagements during the civil war, including Brunete, Teruel, Aragon, and Ebro.

During the 1937 Asturias campaign, one pilot, Adolf Galland, experimented with new bombing tactics. He dropped all bombs on the enemy from every aircraft at the same time for maximum effect. This technique would eventually be picked up by the entire Legion and become known as carpet bombing.

Mussolini committed troops on the ground in order to overthrow a democratically elected government, they were sending a statement to the international community about the political intentions of their respective countries. When Britain and France failed to step in and check this power play, they undermined their own international position and emboldened Hitler to make more dramatic moves toward eastern expansion. Though their intervention would probably not have deterred Hitler's quest for a Nazi empire, it would have shown a clearer and more determined resolve against the spread of Fascism. It is then not surprising that Hitler would assume that if Britain and France would not assist Spain in 1936, they would continue their policy of nonintervention with Czechoslovakia in 1938 and later Poland in 1939.

Britain and France's alliance with the Soviet Union was also severely damaged during this period. The main reason behind Britain and France's failure to support Republicans was their Communist backing. Such blatant rejection of what was now the core belief system of the Soviet Union made Stalin increasingly unwilling to cooperate with the Western powers, and their apparent military weakness in the face of Fascism further convinced Stalin that accommodation with Hitler was necessary. Once Hitler had access to Spanish resources via a pro-Fascist government, he finally had the raw materials necessary for eastern expansion and the accompanying possibility of war.

5

A Haunted Legacy

oday, the body of Generalissimo Francisco Franco lies in a marble tomb in the vast **basilica** of Valle de los Caídos in the Sierra de Guadarrama, near Madrid. The church around him is still as conservatively Catholic as Franco himself and, on the anniversary of the dictator's death, visitors to the church are still checked to ensure that none bring placards or flags associated with the Fascist Party. Even the structure itself carries something of Franco's taint. The imposing and grand building was built by Republican prisoners. Some estimates have around twenty thousand detainees working on the structure from conception to completion. Spain cannot and, since the death of Franco, has not tried to hide its past. However, accepting the past and fully examining the damage are two very different things. As

Opposite: Franco was entombed here, at Valle de los Caídos.

we shall be seen in this chapter, even after Franco had secured Spain for Fascism, there was much to resolve and rebuild.

Effects on Spain

In the immediate aftermath of the Spanish Civil War, Spain's economy was devastated. Ten to fifteen percent of its national wealth had been destroyed and **per capita** household incomes were 28 percent lower in 1939 than they were in 1935. As is common with most wars, the national treasury was depleted. This situation has been particularly aggravated by the Soviet Union's demands that its military aid be purchased with gold.

To add insult to injury, Stalin had convinced the Republican government to ship the majority of its remaining gold reserves to Moscow for "safekeeping." Needless to say, this stock of over 500 tons (454 metric tons) of gold was never returned. The Soviet Union would continue to ignore Spain's requests for its return for decades, hiding behind the excuse that the Communist union could not politically exchange with a Fascist nation. Thus, Spain's economy would continue to suffer throughout the twentieth century, partly due to this loss and partly due to economic mismanagement.

In terms of labor and **infrastructure**, 70 percent of Madrid's factory machinery was in need of replacement and its communications systems, such as the city's tram network, were damaged beyond repair. Roughly one-third of its merchant shipping was out of action, and inflation soared. As Franco had reversed the second Spanish republic's land reforms, agricultural economy remained ineffective and inefficient. Laborers were forced to tolerate periodic unemployment, and landowners continued to refuse modernizations that would cost more in the short term. In addition, the high death toll of the war meant that there was a crippling lack of skilled workers and a huge general labor shortage.

Internationally, Spain was facing massive debts. The country attempted to find foreign loans for investment, but both Britain and Germany demanded that the debt be paid back before further investment would be offered. Germany was especially keen that the cost of its aid during the conflict was returned. Some historians have argued that it was in fact the threat and final outbreak of World War II that gave Spain the financial break it so desperately needed. Franco appears to have attempted to gain leverage over Spain's debt to Britain and France by offering to remain neutral during the ensuing war. There were also discussions with the Germans in November and December 1939, presumably to offer a similar deal. When war did break out, Britain and France finally changed their position and signed trade agreements with Spain in early 1940.

Yet Spain's troubles were not quite over. German exploitation of Spanish resources throughout World War II weakened the country's economic position. The original debt owed to Britain, France, and the United States was not forgotten, and this lever gave the three countries influence in Franco's politics. Its neutral position may have been nationally necessary during World War II, but upon its conclusion, it

After Franco's victory, Republican supporters faced persecution and violence. Here, Franco's troops search a house in Burgos, Spain.

was left isolated within Europe and viewed with suspicion by all sides.

In 1946, the country suffered famine. With its industrial output at a level below that of 1918, it was finally the aid of the right-wing Argentine leader Juan Perón that allowed the Spanish economy to gain some stability. As the Cold War between the United States and the Soviet Union grew in political force, Spain became less and less isolated. After some moderate reforms during the 1950s and 1960s, the country was finally able to develop a powerful capitalist economy. It industrialized and developed a strong service industry.

Politics and Society

Franco remained in power until his death in 1975 and ruled, as described by writer Paul Preston, "as if it were a country occupied by a victorious foreign army." However, despite the continued suffering of Spain's people, to the outside world, the country was able to maintain a facade of peace and security in the immediate years after the Spanish Civil War. The suppression of political opposition and the enforced silence around the horrors of the conflict resulted in a period of seeming political stability. Such was the extent of state repression and the fear it generated that Spain silenced itself and appeared to external eyes to be more unified than ever before.

One key outcome of the war was the status of the Catholic Church in Spanish life. Nearly seven thousand priests and members of religious orders were killed during the conflict; however, once Franco established full control over the country, the Church regained its previous dominant position. It retook control of national education and made itself once again the ultimate authority on family life and morality. Divorce was once again banned in Spain.

Nevertheless, the eventual defeat of the Fascist powers in World War II left Franco extremely vulnerable. He faced increasing pressure from monarchists within his country. He finally agreed to restore the king but significantly kept himself as head of state. Yet, the society that had brought Franco to power was itself changing rapidly. Spain had already lost most of the empire, and in 1956 its last colony, Morocco, gained independence. Without an empire to administrate or any real external or internal threat, Spain's army became essentially defunct—a relic that seemed to have outgrown

FASCISM

Fascism is a form of radical authorial nationalism. It first came to prominence in the early twentieth century in Europe. Most historians have argued that it originated in Italy during World War I and later spread to other European countries. Fascists essentially believe that liberal democracy is obsolete and that the best possible method for social organization is under a totalitarian one-party state. This, so they believe, would ensure strong leadership and clear decisive action in the field of military and economic action. Such societies are most often led by dictators or martial governments. Its followers also reject the notion that violence is inherently negative and instead view it as a tool to achieve national progress.

World War I had a dynamic impact upon Fascism. Many viewed its upheaval as bringing revolutionary changes in war, society, the state, and technology. The war allowed for the rise of a powerful state that could command millions of citizens to serve on the front lines, provide economic production and logistics, and many governments were given unprecedented authority to shape the lives of its populace. Fascists saw these changes as the rise of a new era in politics and social organization.

After World War II, the concept began to shift and evolve into what is now known as neo-Fascism. This form of Fascism involves elements of ultra-nationalism and populism, often with a focus on anti-immigration policies and hostility toward liberal democracy. As of October 2014, there are no countries considered Fascists according to typical definitions; however, there are a number with active neo-Fascist movements or representations in national politics, such as France's Front National and Denmark's Danish People's Party. Many consider the regime of Syrian leader Bashar al-Assad to be Fascist due to its emphasis on state protection and use of extreme violence against its citizens.

its relevance and usefulness. The army quickly lost the social status it had held for so long.

From the 1960s onwards, Franco delegated more and more control, but in many ways it was too little too late. The civil war and Nationalist victory had left Spain a country "frozen in time." No modernization took place within the country for the thirty-six years of Franco's regime, and the rest of Europe would continue to shun Spain until Franco's death in 1975, when democracy was once again restored.

Effects on Europe and Beyond

One of the greatest effects that the Spanish Civil War would have on Germany was the military lessons that Hitler would gain from aiding Franco in the conflict. He discovered the dramatic importance of air power: firstly in the initial transportation of Franco's troops and secondly in the brutal effectiveness of air support for ground troops using blitzkrieg tactics. The Germans were also able to test out their new military developments, such as bullet-resistant fuel tanks, and made important technical discoveries, such as the need for radio contact for armored vehicles. Such lessons were a key part of Hitler's success in his 1939–1940 European campaign.

The war succeeded in bringing Germany and Italy into a much closer political alliance due to their shared Fascist values. It also prevented a reconciliation between Britain, France, and Italy. In April 1935, the French prime minister Pierre Laval, British prime minister Ramsay MacDonald,

Mussolini's political alliance with Germany crucially changed the power dynamic within Europe.

and Italian prime minister Benito Mussolini had signed the Stresa Front agreement in Stresa, Italy. The goal of the agreement was to bind the political friendships between the three countries and to jointly commit to resisting any future attempts by Germany to change the Treaty of Versailles. The pact quickly broke down just two months later, however, when Italy invaded Abyssinia, also known as the Ethiopian Empire. After the Spanish Civil War, Italy's allegiance to Fascism and friendship with Nazi Germany ended all possibility of a reconciliation and ensured Germany a powerful ally for future conflict.

As Britain and France continued their policies of nonintervention and **appeasement**, in a fervent attempt to prevent yet another world war, Germany's position grew in power. Hitler placed Germany as the principal country "defending the world from Communism." Britain and France's "weakness" made Hitler look like a strong and dynamic leader in contrast.

Germany and Italy's cooperation also helped to remove an obstacle from Hitler's path: that of Italy itself. As Stephen Lee explains in *Aspects of European History 1789–1980*:

> 66
>
> *Cooperation between Italy and Germany had far-reaching consequences, the most important of which was the removal of Italian constraint of Hitler's policy of expansion in Central Europe. Although he had clearly indicated in* Mein Kampf *that he intended to construct a Greater Germany, Hitler had been impeded by Mussolini's own interests in Austria. Military involvement in Spain, however, absorbed Mussolini's attention, allowing Hitler to carry out, without Italian opposition, the* **annexation** *of Austria in 1938.*
>
> 99

Germany was determined to avenge itself for the humiliation of the post–World War I **armistice** mandates. The provisions of the Treaty of Versailles had not only punished Germany but also restrained its ability to rearm. Still smarting from the blow, the country would have one of the most formidable armies in Europe by the outbreak of World War II. The French, still believing themselves to be Europe's military superior, would receive a rude awakening when Germany invaded in 1940. Improved German military prowess would also catch the Soviet Union's eye, impressing it with the new power of Germany, and forcing it to carefully consider its next diplomatic steps.

Britain and France

The Spanish Civil War proved to the British that "the bomber will always get through" and seemed to give more credibility to a policy of appeasement. The countries of France and Britain still firmly believed that World War I was and should have been the "war to end all wars." At the 1919 League of Nations peace conference in Versailles, there had been diplomatic agreements never again to allow such a cataclysmic event to occur. The sheer scale of suffering experienced by the Spanish people made it clear to the British government that another large-scale European war would bring new horrors in numbers exceeding that of World War I. The lack of political similitude between the different foreign intervention forces lent further support for appeasement. Many politicians argued that it was better to let the opposing factions battle it out and exhaust one another rather than dragging democratic countries into the fight. Democratic European countries still believed that Communism was the greater threat, and so they could not assist the Republicans in allowing Communism to gain a foothold in Spain.

In addition to these wider concerns, Britain was experiencing its own series of crises. The British economy was floundering after the 1929 Wall Street crash in the United States and unemployment was at a record high. In 1936, the newly crowned Edward VIII abdicated the throne of England in order to marry his American mistress, leaving the country in a state of shock and confusion. The British Empire was also beginning to feel its foundations being shaken as independence protests in India became increasingly violent. Britain was desperate to find any excuse not to engage in warfare.

However, Britain's policies of appeasement and their lack of action in Spain led Hitler to change his perception of Britain. His initial plans had been to avoid a war and attempt to ally himself with the British, based on a belief that racially Germany and Britain were the most closely aligned. However, by 1938, Hitler had begun to lose respect for Britain and the country's attempts to avert war instead encouraged the German dictator to further heights of aggression.

The USSR

The Soviet Union was the first totalitarian state after World War I. In 1917, Vladimir Lenin seized power in what became known as the Russian Revolution. When he died in January 1924, there was no clear path of succession. Though the obvious choice for many was Leon Trotsky, head of the military revolutionary committee that had sparked the revolution, he was also disliked by an equally large number of

Stalin's support of the Republicans was both lackluster and haphazard. Here, he poses circa 1930.

party members. He and fellow party member Joseph Stalin became embroiled in a conflict for ultimate leadership for almost three years before Stalin took full control. During the 1930s, Stalin's main goal was to eliminate all barriers to a complete and unquestioned use of his own power.

In 1933, he created the Central Purge Commission to publicly investigate and put on trial members of the Communist Party accused of treason. Between 1933 and 1934, over one hundred thousand members were expelled from the party, and over the next four years thousands were arrested or shot, including roughly 25 percent of the army officer corps. During the 1934 Communist Party Congress, 1,108 of the 1,966 delegates were arrested, and 98 members of the Central Committee were executed. By the time Franco declared victory in Spain, Stalin's one and only concern was the preservation of his power and ideologies at any cost.

In this light, it was not only Republicans who experienced defeat in Spain, but to an extent Communism itself. The Nationalist victory hugely undermined the international credibility of Communism on the world stage. In addition, Stalin's meager contributions to the Republican cause had in fact created further divisions within the left wing and disillusioned many former Soviet supporters. Their cynical involvement caused a huge loss of intellectual sympathy for the USSR within the West, and this would have further ramifications upon World War II.

While the Spanish Civil War had exacerbated the hostility between the USSR and Germany, it also pushed Soviet foreign policy away from an alliance with the Western powers with the aim of containing Germany. Instead, it was recalibrated to one of Nazi appeasement. Britain and France's actions had convinced Stalin that neither would be a reliable ally against German expansion, and Stalin began to show interest in a possible Nazi-Soviet deal as early as December 1937. Stalin's convictions in this direction were strengthened when Britain sacrificed Czechoslovakia to Hitler's expansionist dreams and allowed Germany to **annex** the Sudetenland area in September 1938.

In August 1939, Hitler and Stalin would sign a pact of non-aggression. The agreement was negotiated by the Soviet foreign minister Vyacheslav Molotov and German foreign minister Joachim von Ribbentrop. While officially only a non-aggression treaty, the document also contained a secret protocol that divided the whole of Eastern Europe into German- and Soviet-controlled areas, with the USSR receiving "rights" over Latvia, Estonia, Finland, Lithuania, and eastern Poland. The agreement was reached only days after the breakdown of military talks with Britain and France to build a Franco-Anglo-Soviet alliance against Hitler.

The United States

During the 1930s, the United States Congress passed the Neutrality Acts in an effort to protect itself from the growing unrest in Europe and Asia. They were also prompted in part by growing noninterventionist and isolationist sentiment within the country. After the huge costs of American involvement in World War I, the country was not keen to return to war. Powerful Republican senators, such as William Edgar Borah and Arthur H. Vandenberg, were extremely vocal in their support for noninterventionism, and the Democratic representative Louis Ludlow attempted without success to pass an amendment requiring a public referendum before any declaration of war several times between 1935 and 1940.

Although horrified by the atrocities committed by both sides during the Spanish Civil War, the United States remained neutral throughout the conflict and offered no tangible assistance. In fact, the war strengthened the United States' determination to remain isolationist. However, the acts themselves were often unclear and highly problematic. They made no distinctions between aggressor and victim, and in fact would later limit the United States' ability to aid Britain and France against Nazi Germany. President Franklin D. Roosevelt was himself extremely critical of the acts, aware of the restrictions they would place on the administration's ability to help allies. However, facing reelection, Roosevelt felt he could not ignore the demands of Southern voters and the anger of public opinion at that time. As a result, he reluctantly signed the Neutrality Acts into law.

On October 5, 1937, Roosevelt delivered what became known as the quarantine speech. He called upon the international community to "quarantine [against the] epidemic of lawlessness" shown by aggressive Fascist nations, instead of following the American neutrality and nonintervention policies prevalent at the time. However, this act only intensified nonintervention sentiment nationally. Many American citizens protested against the notion of becoming involved in another European war. Though no countries were mentioned in the speech, it was widely assumed to refer to Japan, Italy, and Germany. Roosevelt argued for the use of economic pressure rather than outright aggression. However, words meant very little to the European dictators and military regime in Japan. The Neutrality Acts were repealed in 1941 after a German submarine attack on American vessels and the Japanese attack on Pearl Harbor.

After the completion of World War II, Spain was still feeling the chill of European isolation. In 1946, the United Nations called for economic sanctions against Franco. Its member states followed suit by breaking off diplomatic relations with the country. Spain was similarly excluded from the United States' postwar economic recovery package for Europe, also known as Marshall Aid. The West hoped that, given time, Spain would experience another crisis, which would eventually force Franco from power.

Relations between Spain and the United States continued in the same fashion until a greater threat appeared on its horizon: the burgeoning Cold War with the USSR. Though Franco was undoubtedly Fascist, he was clearly a strong anti-Communist force. In the spirit of "the enemy of my enemy is my friend," the United States started to cultivate friendlier relations with Spain. When the Cold War became global in 1950, the United States transformed these new ties into direct economic action. In 1950, President Dwight D. Eisenhower gave permission for the American grant to Spain, and in return Americans were given access to Spanish air bases. Spain became an official ally of the United States, and in 1955, it joined the United Nations.

Effects of the War Today

Today, the Spanish Civil War still remains a painful and complex subject in Spain. In 2007, steps were taken to address and heal the wounds of the war and the subsequent dictatorship. Under the leadership of Prime Minister José Luis Rodríguez Zapatero, the Spanish Socialist Workers' Party government proposed the Law of Historical Memory. The bill formally condemned Franco's dictatorship and honored

BRINGING UP THE BODIES

After Franco's death, the Spanish government approved the 1977 Amnesty Law (Ley de Amnistia de 1977). This granted pardon for all political crimes committed by Nationalist and Republican supporters during the Spanish Civil War and the subsequent White Terror. Concrete figures of the dead do not exist. This is partly due to the Francoist government destroying thousands of documents relating to the White Terror, forging certificates of release when in fact men were taken out and executed, and severely disfiguring corpses so as to be unrecognizable to grieving families.

Nevertheless, in 2008, Spanish judge Balthasar Garzón, of the National Court of Spain authorized the first ever investigation into the disappearance of over one hundred thousand victims of Franco's regime between 1936 and 1952. The preliminary inquest was granted on the grounds that mass murder constituted a crime against humanity and as such was not subject to any amnesty or statute of limitations.

Just two years later, Garzón was accused by the government of violating the terms of the amnesty and his jurist powers were suspended. However, the same year, an Argentine court reopened the case. Amnesty International, Human Rights Watch, the Council of Europe, and the United Nations have all requested the Spanish government to investigate the crimes of Franco's dictatorship, but so far to little effect.

the victims of both the civil war and the Francoist regime. In addition, it provided definitive reparation and recognition for victims, as well as new legal opportunities. The bill declared that arbitrary sentences delivered by Franco's military courts were "unjust" and "illegitimate." By doing so, it offered victims and their families the ability to seek redress through courts for executions, exile, and persecution by the regime's operatives. Token compensation was also offered for families of those wounded or killed under Franco's dictatorship. The bill was created after many months of negotiation and argument with the conservative Popular Party (PP). Its supporters lauded its arrival as an act of symbolic justice and a sign that Spain was finally beginning to address the demons of its past. However, there were also many critics. The PP attacked the bill as a political weapon designed not only to rake up the past and reopen old wounds but also as a form of political propaganda. Left-wing critics also condemned the bill, but for being too soft. They pointed out its lack of provisions for a census of the tens of thousands killed by Franco's troops and buried anonymously. The most recent conservative Popular Party government, led by Mariano Rajoy, who assumed office in December 2011, has not repealed or amended the law; however, they have taken efforts to curtail state help to exhume victims.

While the Spanish Civil War was not the ultimate cause of World War II, it did hold a lynchpin position within the interwar period. In one sense it acted as a smaller-scale battleground for the two ideologies of Fascism and

Prime Minister José Luis Rodríguez Zapatero's administration was the first to address the horrific acts committed under the Franco regime.

Communism, where each side struggled to show the rest of the world its dominance. There is also some credence to the idea that Spain was a taste test of World War II. It gave Nazi and Italian forces the opportunity to exercise new military technology and strategy, created new alliances and abandoned others, introduced and adjusted military tactics, and evolved and inspired diplomacy. Similarly, the inability or refusal to act was equally crucial in determining how the next war would be fought. Nonintervention only encouraged further aggression, and isolation weakened economies rather than protected them. As such, the Spanish Civil War was not simply a traumatic and defining conflict but a prophecy for Europe that both warned of future threats and laid the board for future players.

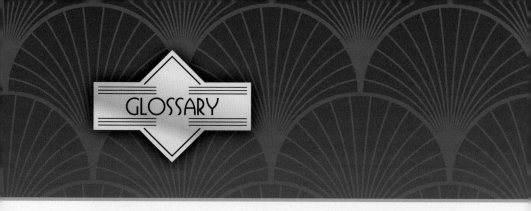

GLOSSARY

agrarian Relating to agriculture or land tenure.

anarchist A person who believes in the abolition of the government as necessary for full social and political liberty.

annex To incorporate a territory into the domain of a city, country, or state.

anticlerical Opposing the influence and activities of the Church in public affairs.

appeasement To yield or concede to aggressive demands in order to maintain peaceful relations.

armistice A truce or temporary suspension of hostilities by warring parties.

basilica A type of Catholic church that has been granted special privileges by the pope.

blitzkrieg A swift and intensive military attack using tanks supported by aircraft.

Bolshevik A member of the Russian Communist Party post-1918.

brainchild A product of creative work or thought.

Carlist A supporter of the Spanish political movement that sought to establish a different line of the Bourbon dynasty, descended from Count of Molina Don Carlos, to the throne.

colonial The control or governing influence of one country over a dependent country, nation, or territory.

Cortes The two houses of Spain's national legislative body.

counterrevolution A revolution against a government recently established by revolution.

deposition The act of removing a monarch from a throne; forced removal.

enlightenment An eighteenth-century philosophical movement promoting human reasons and advancements in science and education.

Germanophile A person who is interested in or studies about Germany and German culture.

guerrilla Irregular soldiers that harass enemies using surprise raids, sabotaging communication and supply lines, etc.

incense To become intensely angry.

indoctrinate To be instructed in an ideology with a specifically biased belief or point of view.

inflation A persistent, substantial rise in prices due to an increase in the volume of money in a country.

infrastructure The fundamental facilities and systems serving a country, city, or area, such as public transportation.

interned The restriction or confinement of a person within a camp as a prisoner of war or enemy.

peninsular An area of land almost completely surrounded by water except for a small area connecting it to the mainland.

per capita By or for each individual person.

shock troops Troops especially trained and equipped for engaging in assault.

totalitarian A centralized government that does not tolerate parties of differing opinion and exercises control over both public and private life.

ultra-conservatism Extremely politically conservative.

1936

February Popular Front wins national elections and Azaña is appointed president of Spain.

March The right-wing Falange Party is banned.

March to May Military uprisings occur in Spanish Morocco and some parts of mainland Spain.

July The government dissolves the regular army. July 19, Franco arrives to take command of the army in Morocco. Hitler agrees to help the Nationalists. Stalin agrees to help the Republicans. German and Italian planes airlift Franco's army to the Spanish mainland.

August First international brigade volunteers arrive in Spain.

September Franco becomes as head of state and head of the armed forces of Spain.

October The first aid from Russia arrives for the Republicans.

November Germany and Italy recognize Franco as head of Spain's government.

1937

February Nationalists start a major offensive against Madrid. International brigades play an important part in resisting this offensive.

March Battle of Guadalajara. Italian "volunteers" are defeated. This leads to Franco abandoning any attempt to take Madrid.

April Guernica is destroyed by aerial bombing.

May Republican groups in Barcelona argue, causing serious weaknesses in the city.

June The strategic city of Bilboa falls to the Nationalists.

August The Vatican recognizes Franco's regime.

1938

April Republican Spain is split in two by the Nationalists.

May Franco declares that the Republicans have to unconditionally surrender.

July Start of the collapse of the Republican army after the Battle of the Ebro.

October International brigades leave Spain.

1939

January Barcelona falls to Franco.

February Britain and France recognize the legitimacy of Franco's government.

March Madrid surrenders to Franco.

April Republicans surrender unconditionally to Franco.

Books

Bolloten, Burnett. *The Spanish Civil War: Revolution and Counterrevolution*. Chapel Hill, NC: The University of North Carolina Press, 2015.

Casanova, Julian. *A Short History of the Spanish Civil War*. London, UK: I.B. Taurus, 2014.

Hochschild, Adam. *Spain in Our Hearts: Americans in the Spanish Civil War, 1936–1939*. London, UK: Pan Macmillan, 2016.

Websites

The *Guardian*: War of Ideas

https://www.theguardian.com/books/2007/feb/17/historybooks.featuresreviews

This online article from the *Guardian* newspaper examines the contribution of artists and writers to the historical perception of the war.

Spanish Wars: The Civil War

http://www.spanishwars.net/20th-century-spanish-civil-war.html

This is a breakdown of events within the context of Spanish history. It also includes resources about Spanish conflicts by century.

Spartacus Educational: The Spanish Civil War

http://spartacus-educational.com/Spanish-Civil-War.htm

This website explores a range of factors relating to the Spanish Civil War, including main events and issues, political and military organizations involved, and breakdowns of major battles and international involvement.

Videos and Radio

In Our Time: The Spanish Civil War

http://www.bbc.co.uk/programmes/p00548wn

This online history radio program discusses the causes and consequences of the war with a panel of academic experts on the conflict.

The Spanish Civil War: Prelude to Tragedy

https://www.youtube.com/watch?v=Lu5f9hp0IP4

Here is the first episode of a documentary series charting the progress of the war.

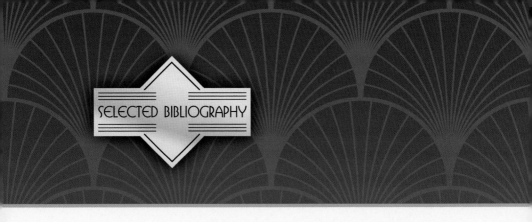

Alpert, M. *A New International History of the Spanish Civil War: Second Edition*. Basingstoke, UK: Palgrave Macmillan, 2004.

Basilio, Miriam. *Visual Propaganda, Exhibitions, and the Spanish Civil War*. Farnham, UK: Ashgate Publishing Limited, 2014.

Beevor, Anthony. *The Battle for Spain: The Spanish Civil War 1936-1939*. London, UK: Machete UK, 2012.

Forrest, Andrew. *The Spanish Civil War*. London, UK: Routledge, 2000.

Hart, Stephen M., ed. *"¡No Pasarán!": Art, Literature and the Spanish Civil War*. London, UK: Tamesis Books Limited, 1988.

Jackson, Michael W. *Fallen Sparrows: The International Brigades in the Spanish Civil War, Volume 212*. Phildelphia, PA: American Philosophical Society, 1994.

Whealey, Robert H. *Hitler and Spain: The Nazi Role in the Spanish Civil War, 1936-1939*. Lexington, KY: The University Press of Kentucky, 2004.

INDEX

Page numbers in **boldface** are illustrations. Entries in **boldface** are glossary terms.

Katie Griffiths is a long-time enthusiast of history from around the world. Her love of different cultures and their stories has taken her to many countries, including China, Japan, and Cambodia. She currently lives in Edinburgh, Scotland. She loves traveling, hiking, and collecting graphic novels in her free time. To learn more and to see her other works, visit http://www.katiegriffiths.org.